THE
SCOTTISH

CAMPBELL, Jimmy Powdrell

The Scottish
crown jewels and the
minister's wife

THE
SCOTTISH CROWN JEWELS
AND THE
MINISTER'S WIFE

JIMMY POWDRELL CAMPBELL

TEMPUS

First published 2007

Tempus Publishing
Cirencester Road, Chalford
Stroud, Gloucestershire, GL6 8PE
www.tempus-publishing.com

Tempus Publishing is an imprint of NPI Media Group

British Library Cataloguing in Publication Data.
A catalogue record for this book is available from the British Library.

ISBN 978 0 7524 4029 3

Typesetting and origination by NPI Media Group
Printed and bound in Great Britain

Contents

About the Author

Jimmy Powdrell Campbell is an historian and composer. He scripted and assisted in production of a BBC Radio Scotland dramatised documentary based on his research on the Scottish Crown Jewels. He has researched several areas of Scottish history, has participated in many BBC documentaries and contributed to various radio and TV programmes. He lives in Stirlingshire.

List of Illustrations

Preface

A few years ago I made a phone call to a respected Scottish repository of knowledge which I won't name: 'I'm looking for any information you might have on Christian Fletcher ... ' The answer I got pretty much says it all: 'Oh, I don't think we have anything on the Bounty here.' This is a story that is hardly ever told outside of a small area of north-east Scotland, and what you hear there is often a long way from the truth of it: Cromwell had occupied Scotland; the Crown Jewels were lodged in Dunnottar Castle; while the English troops had the castle under siege, the Regalia were lowered down the side of the rock to a serving woman who had been coming about collecting seaweed and she took them to a small church further down the coast where they were buried by the minister's wife and there they remained until the restoration of the monarchy.

Another version tells that the minister's wife, Christian Fletcher, went to the castle and carried the Regalia away under her winter clothing, passing right through the Cromwellian camp as she left the castle, before riding back to the church. It's not giving too much away to say that this is the true story but, until quite recently, getting at the truth has proved to be next to impossible, the reason being not only a lack of good documentation but, frankly, the number of extraordinary, blatant lies that had been told by some of those who had been involved.

In 1896, edited by Charles Howden, the Scottish Historical Society published (Vol. 26) 'Papers Relative to the Preservation of the Honours of Scotland', but the most in-depth, comprehensive account and largest collection of relevant documentation was and remains the 1910 publication, *In Defence of the Regalia 1651-2* by the Rev. Douglas Gordon Barron.

The Rev. Barron, who had assisted with the 1896 publication, presented extensive documentation including papers from:

The family papers of the Ogilvies of Barras (George Ogilvy of Barras was the governor of Dunnottar Castle during the Cromwellian occupation).

Papers now held by Aberdeen University, Special Libraries and Archives: Keith-Falconer family, earls of Kintore.

Manuscript Collections now held by National Library of Scotland: Papers of the Keith family, Earls Marschal and Murray family, baronets, of Ochtertyre (ref: Acc 6026, 11041) – William Keith was the owner of Dunnottar and, as Earl Marschal of Scotland, individually responsible for the Crown Jewels.

The Scottish Historical Review, Vol. 4.

The Bannatyne Club 'Papers Relative to the Regalia of Scotland.'

Papers in the possession of the Rev. William Disney Innes of Cowie.

The Bodleian Library: the Clarendon Manuscripts, 43 ff. 44, 60, 73, 107, 139.

Marschal College, Aberdeen: Papers Relative to the Union of the Parliaments deposited in 1709 by William 9th Earl Marschall (copy of Christian Fletcher's 'Information').

The Rev. Barron's *In Defence of the Regalia* was a monumental, painstaking work of research but one or two important pieces of the jigsaw were simply unavailable in 1910. It is now possible, for the first time, to tell the true story of the Scottish Crown Jewels and the minister's wife and, accordingly, thanks are due. Firstly, to the late Rev. Barron, to Liz Brown of the Historic Manuscripts Commission, to Edinburgh University Library Special Collections, and also to an Edinburgh bookseller and antiquarian by the name of David Laing.

Edinburgh University Library describe David Laing in the following terms: 'An antiquary, editor of older texts and an inveterate collector of books and manuscripts, he was appointed Librarian of the Signet Library in 1837, holding the post until his death in 1878.' His collection, they say, is 'the most important manuscripts donation in the Library's history.' Laing, it seems, was in the habit of buying all manner of old documents, often family papers that had been passed down through the generations. One handful of letters purchased by him at auction had originally been the property of James Grainger, minister at Kinneff and his wife, Christian Fletcher. The family had kept these letters for two centuries and that correspondence, primarily between James Grainger and the Dowager Countess of Marschall, held the key to this story that has defied all attempts to uncover the truth since 1660.

Before moving on to the story, I feel I should warn everyone that I have taken some atrocious liberties with the text of many of the seventeenth-century documents, for which I am not about to apologise. While taking all possible care to retain the original meaning, I have standardised the spelling and replaced some of the more obscure words, abbreviations and phrasing with the modern equivalent. Occasionally, it does spoil the text, especially where there is no modern English word that adequately expresses the meaning, as is still so often the case with the Scots language. 'But ye so vilipendit or adwyse and slichtit ye busines of so hie concernment ...' was butchered to read: 'But you thought so little of our advice and slighted the business of so high concern ...'. It could have been left untouched with a note explaining that 'to vilipend' means to show contempt by one's actions, but it soon becomes a tedious read and it gets in the way of the story.

Just to reassure anyone who might feel they're being denied the pleasure of reading the original transcripts — which, it can't be denied, has its own fascination — here is a random sample of what you are missing:

George Ogilvy [Governor of Dunnottar Castle] to my Lord Balcarras.
My Lord, Yours I receavit and ane letter frome the comitie of estats to your lo. daitit the tenth of Sepr qrin they desyr your lo. to hau ane cair for securing of the honors and the king stuiffs qlk wes in donor. bot no order to your lo. for remouing of the samen nor to me for the delyuery of them bot as I doe presaue is raider to hau takine courss wt this houss qr they ar to hau furnest the samen wt both wittolls and men and euery

thing niedfull as the securest part nou in this part of the kingdome, bot gin the comitie of estats quhos hands is at this letter sall aney way think otherways I reuerence ther better jugment and sall upone the receat of ane order frome them wt ane exoneration to my lord marchall and me delyuer them to aney hauing that warrand qlk I hop will giu your lo. full satisfactio. for bot ther particular order I can not dou it being ane busines of such gryt importance, and I hop your lo. will pardoune me for that and in the mane tyme that your lo. wald be plessit to causs prowyd us of wittolls for as your lo. knous ther wes ane order derectit frome the comitie of estats to the generall comisser for to hau sent heir sax hundreth bolls of meill qrof we hau not receavit the halff yrof and nou as I ame informit they hau sold and disponed the samen at Abd. and the schyr of the mernes qlk sould hau peyit mantinence to us will not acknowlerg us ane peney as your lo. may presaue be ther ansur to me qlk your lo. sall receave heir incloissit so I think we ar in ane very hard conditione and I think gin thes honors wer remoue, non sould dou so much as once ask for us, bot I hop your lo. for the respeck ye carey to my lord Marschall will tak this to your consideratiô and let us be suplied of such things as we stand in nied of for since I hau ane particular order frome the king for keiping of this hous and since your lo. hauing the pour in your hands wt the comitie of estats I hop spedie courss sal be takine about the prowyding of this houss for gin your lo. and the comitie wald prowyd me wt ane hundreth men qrof I hau receauit non as yet excep fourtie & so long as I hau wittolls or amunitione I sall mantine the samen wnder God aganest all Ingland So not willing to trubill your lo. forder bot that I ame your lo. most humbill seruant – George Ogilvy.

Acknowledgements

Having already expressed, albeit inadequately, thanks to Edinburgh University Library, and to Liz Hart of the Historical Manuscripts Commission, without whose help there would have been no story to tell, I would like also to gratefully acknowledge the invaluable assistance of the Very Rev. Dr Finlay A.J. Macdonald, Principal Clerk to the General Assembly of the Church of Scotland, for his having graciously provided access to the records of the Church of Scotland; and to thank Dr Lionel K.J. Glassey, M.A., D.Phil., F.R.Hist.S., Senior Lecturer, Dept History, Glasgow University, for giving up his weekend to provide much-needed help in palaeography. Grateful thanks are due also to Dr Norman H. Reid, Keeper of Manuscripts and Muniments at The Library of the University of St Andrews, to many members of the staff of The National Archives of Scotland, The National Library of Scotland, the University of Glasgow, as also to the staff and proprietors of Dunecht Estates (Dunnottar Castle), to the Kinneff Old Church Preservation Trust and to Risto Hurmalainen for his photo of Dunnottar Castle reproduced on the front cover (all the way from Finland).

Last but most definitely not least, special thanks to Kirsteen and to her husband, who prefers to remain nameless, for their support, their time, and their much-appreciated assistance.

Chapter One

Londoners in the seventeenth century were no strangers to public executions but this was history in the making. At Whitehall, on the morning of 30 January 1649, they watched, transfixed, the fascinating spectacle of a monarch laying his head on the block. Moments earlier, Charles I had inspired more admiration than envy amongst the onlookers by declaring that he was going from a corruptible to an incorruptible crown. They watched him stretch out his arms to indicate that he was ready to die and, with one swing of the axe, it was over.

Charles had never really had any sense of the power that he had taken on. It attracted moderates and radicals alike to its cause but it fed on death, misery and destruction, and it was insatiable. Anything that smacked of the slightest remnant of Catholicism had to be sought out, crushed, ground into the dirt where it belonged. Anyone who thought otherwise was in league with the Devil; anyone who thought at all was in league with the Devil. The religious fanaticism of the English Puritans was more than enough to bring merry England to a miserable end but it was almost fun-loving, benevolent and tolerant when compared to that of the Calvinist Scots.

The small kingdom of Scotland had long since declared the Roman Catholic Church an enemy of God and of the State, and when it came to hatred and intolerance, the Scottish Calvinists could put Oliver Cromwell in the shade, so it had really come as a bit of a shock to them when Cromwell completely ignored their wishes and beheaded their king. Charles may have been a 'malignant' but he was a Stewart; he was still the King of Scotland. Was the Scottish nation now expected to become a subordinate territory of an English republic? Well … yes.

Arguably, the Scots had brought it upon themselves. As far back as 1637, Charles I and the Scots had been on a collision course. The days when monarchs had anything like a realistic sense of self-worth were long past and Charles had been brought up to believe that the king was born to be the head of the Church. That had been the deal when Henry VIII was persuaded of the expediency of abandoning the Roman Catholic faith. Elizabeth had had no problem establishing herself in the role and, of course, Charles's father, James I and VI of Scotland, had put his own name to the Holy Book. Charles believed that kings ruled by God-given right and, as King of Scotland, he believed that the monarch's authority over the Scottish Church was bound to be universally accepted. All he had done, as he saw it, was to try to introduce a more Anglican-style service. In the event, it was like poking a stick into a wasps' nest. The Calvinists were beside themselves with righteous fury. They saw it as Catholic ritual in disguise. Riots were organised and the rabble were whipped into a frenzy of hatred. As always, those with the least spiritual dimension to their personalities were the most incensed and the most vehement in their opposition to this imagined heresy.

Religion was an excitable business in those days. Armed with the Old Testament, a handful of spiritually impoverished men were able to impose their dominance and their personal will on a nation, in the name of God. As an instrument of oppression, Christ's name was invoked at every opportunity but they preached, rather, from their own painful interpretation of the texts that had preceded Christianity. Every manner of seething unconscious resentment and commonplace neurotic antipathy was sanctified by religious rhetoric and by 1640, eighty years after the Reformation Parliament, those many Catholic families who still refused to comply were subject to increasingly severe pressure to bow to the Protestant Church.

The Domestic Annals of Scotland tells the tale of the Presbytery's efforts to convert the Marquis of Douglas and his wife, a daughter of the first Marquis of Huntly:

For many years past, the presbytery of Lanark had acted as an inquisition over them, sending deputations every now and then to Douglas

Castle, to deal with them for their conversion, intermeddling with their domestic affairs, and threatening them with excommunication if they did not speedily give 'satisfaction.' With great difficulty, and after many conferences, they had prevailed on the Lady Marquess to attend the parish church, and allow her children to be instructed in the Presbyterian catechism: a mere external conformity, of course, but involving a homage to the system which seems to have pleased the ecclesiastical authorities.

It took six years to bring the marquis to an inclination to abjure popery and sign the Covenant; and great was the rejoicing when he performed this ceremony before the parish congregation. A moderator of presbytery reported his 'great contentment' in seeing his lordship communicate and give attentive ear to the sermons. Seeing, however, that the lady remained immovable, the reverend court deemed it necessary to demand of the noble pair that their children should be secluded from them, in order that assurance might be had of their being brought up in the Protestant religion. This seems to have been too much for the old peer. He plainly broke through all engagements to them, by going and joining the Royalist rebel Montrose.

As his lordship fell into the hands of the Estates, [the Scottish government] by whom he was imprisoned in Dumbarton Castle, the presbytery obtained an increased power over the lady. They now brought her before them, to examine her touching her 'malignancy and obstinate continuance in the profession of popery.' Imagine the daughter of the superb Huntly, the mother of the future head of the chivalric house of Douglas, forced to appear 'with bated breath and whispering humbleness' before the presbytery of Lanark! She really did give them such smooth words as induced them to hold off for a little while. But they soon had occasion once more to bewail the effects of their 'manifold expressions of lenity and long-suffering' towards her, which they saw attended by no effect but 'disobedience.' The process for her excommunication and the taking any of her children was in full career in January 1646; and yet by some means which do not appear, it did not advance.

Meanwhile the marquis had been suffering a long imprisonment for his lapse with Montrose, and his estate was embarrassed with a fine of

50,000 merks. It had become indispensable for the good of his family, that he should be somehow reconciled to the stern powers then ruling. At the beginning of 1647, the descendant of those mail-clad Douglases who in the fifteenth century shook the Scottish throne, was found literally on his knees before the Lanark presbytery, expressing his penitence for breach of covenant, and giving assurance of faithfulness in time to come. The Estates consequently contented themselves with one half of his fine, and an offer of the use of his lands for the quartering of troops, and he was then liberated.

Soon after, he agreed to consign his children to be boarded with the minister of the parish of Douglas, while a young man should attend to act as their preceptor; but the satisfaction produced by this concession was quickly dashed, when the presbytery learned that his lordship was secretly arranging to send his youngest son to be bred in France. It was really a curious game between their honest unsparing zeal on the one hand, and his lordship's craft and territorial consequence on the other. Every now and then we have a peep of the demure lady, not less resolute in adhering to her faith than they were pertinacious in seeking to bring her to the superior light. How the recusant pair must have in secret chafed under the mute acquiescence which they were forced to give, in a rule outraging every sense of natural right, and every feeling of self-respect! With what smothered rage would they view those presbyterial deputations on their approach to Douglas Castle – more formidable than a thousand of the troops of Long shanked Edward had ever been to the good Sir James!

... What are we to think of the conclusion of the affair with the marchioness, when, on the 9th of March 1650, two ministers went to pass upon her that sentence of excommunication which was to make her homeless and an outlaw, unless she should instantly profess the Protestant faith; at the same time telling her 'how fearful a sin it was to swear with equivocation or mental reservation.' The lady of course reflected that the system represented by her visitors was now triumphant over everything – that, for one thing, it had brought her brother Huntly, not a twelvemonth ago, beneath the stroke of the Maiden. She 'declared she had no more doubts,' and at the command of one of the ministers, held up her hand, and solemnly accepted the Covenant before the congregation. 'After he had read the Solemn League and Covenant, and desired her to hold up her hand and swear by the great name of God to observe, according to her power, every article thereof, she did so; and after divine service was ended, he desired her to go to the session-table and subscribe the Covenant, and, before the minister and elders, she went to the said table and did subscribe.'

'Heaven scarce believed the conquest it surveyed,
And saints with wonder heard the vows I made.'

On the very day that this was reported by the two ministers to the presbytery, the court, 'hearing that of late the Marquis of Douglas and his lady had sent away one of their daughters to France, to a popish lady, to be bred with her in popery, without the knowledge of the presbytery, and without any warrant from the Estates, thought the fault intolerable, and so much the more, because they had sent away one of their sons before to the court of France.' For some time after, the reverend presbytery dealt earnestly with the marquis for the withdrawal of his children from France, but without success. They also had occasion to lament that he and his lady rarely attended public worship, and failed to have private exercises at home. Of their own great error in forcing this noble family into hypocritical professions, and interfering so violently with their domestic arrangements, no suspicion seems ever once to have crossed their minds.

It is easy to forget that people have not really changed much in the last thousand years. The firebrands who exercised such fearful power in seventeenth-century Scotland would do so again today, if they could. Democracy protects us, to some extent, from the worst excesses of the ever-present legion of those who would tell us what to think, what to believe, and how to behave, according to their own dismal, narrow view of morality. Then, as now, most people just wanted to get on with their lives, go to their work and come home to their families. Even within the early Presbyterian Church, there were plenty of normal, mentally sound people who had no great desire to set fire to yet another unfortunate accused of witchcraft. Their time would come, but certainly not in this century.

As the records of the Church of Scotland express it:

> The period to which our attention is now directed is one which excites a painful interest. It is pregnant with lessons of infinite value: it presents the most humiliating views of human nature; and, while the hallowed name, and rites, and spirit of religion were desecrated by its pretended votaries – by the clergy of that age, in particular, without distinction of parties – these memorials present to view an incarnation of all the worst passions by which human beings are agitated. Each – for madness ruled the hour – would try its own persuasive power.'

This was a time blighted by the evil of religious extremism where the zeal-driven personalities of a few essentially weak men terrorised the Scottish nation with the wrath of an ill-tempered God who was as mean spirited and vengeful as themselves. Failing the timely intervention of Divine Justice, they gladly meted out their own punishments in lieu. Of course, people had been burning at the stake and suffering the agonies of varying degrees of mutilation and prolonged execution since time immemorial. The Protestant martyrs like Patrick Hamilton and George Wishart suffered at the hands of the Catholic Church in exactly the same way. It was, however, the law itself that had been so completely corrupted. The law of Scotland was now in the hands of a small number of individuals, many of whom could, in the most charitable terms, only be described as disturbed. It was not so much the fact that someone's tongue was to be bored with a red-hot bodkin, someone's ear was to be nailed to the Tron, or someone's wife was to be burnt at the stake; the true horror was the type of people who were deciding what should be considered a punishable offence. They found their guidance in the Bible but their interpretation of the scriptures was thoroughly undermined by the very psychological inadequacies that had attracted them to extreme Calvinism in the first place. In logic, such a system of thought might be described as a circular reference. Their God thought with their thoughts, hated with their hate and, perhaps worst of all, understood with their understanding.

In England, root-and-branch reform of the Church had never seriously been on the agenda. Not to put too fine a point on it, the English Reformation had come about because the King wanted a divorce. The Pope had only recently given Henry VIII the title, Defender of the Faith, because of his thorough opposition to Luther's Protestant ideas. (The tribute must have appealed to his vanity because, incredibly, he saw nothing wrong with keeping the title after being excommunicated from the Church that had conferred it upon him). For England, the Reformation was, primarily, a break with the authority of Rome. To a large extent, the trappings and ceremonies of the Church itself remained the same. The main thing had been that Henry got his divorce. The Act of Supremacy, with Henry supplanting the Pope as the head of the Church was, therefore, pretty much accepted throughout the country as the imposition it was (and the Treasons Act removed any lingering doubts). It was mainly those with family connections to the Catholic Church, and those knights who, in the course of their military careers, had taken oaths of allegiance to the Church, who found themselves in an untenable position, their loyalty and their honour being thoroughly compromised by that all-too-simple solution to the King's marital problems.

Scotland was a different story entirely. The Scottish Reformation had taken place not by royal edict but in direct defiance of the monarch. It was all about religion and their religion was something they took very seriously. They thought about it all the time. They scoured the Bible daily to better understand God's Word and they found that the Lord agreed with everything that they thought themselves. Above all, they found that God hated Catholics.

Charles I had the misfortune to be King of this country at this time and, as often happens with kings, those closest to him were not inclined to tell him what his Scottish subjects really thought of him, how they really felt about a monarch whose spiritual leanings were, in some ways, almost indistinguishable from those of a 'papist' – a term which inferred a disgust worthy only of the lowest forms of life. In those days, especially in the lowlands of Scotland, a man either became a Protestant or he became a social pariah. It was a fear-based culture and, once established, it was self-perpetuating. The fear of being the object of hatred generated an ethos of hatred. Amongst the ordinary people, who had absolutely no power and less inclination to express the slightest hint of dissent, anti-Catholic bigotry, it might be argued, was a means of self-preservation. Both at a conscious and an unconscious level, social acceptance and even personal safety was most assured by making a show of hatred – the more insecure the individual, the greater the show of hatred. Fear generated hatred and hatred generated fear.

Charles, oblivious to the realities of life in Scotland at that time, shared his father's opinion that the Presbyterian system – a Church without bishops – undermined the very foundations of regal sovereignty. The idea of the equality of all under God was, he believed, a recipe for anarchy. Altogether, his views, and his belief in the right of kings to impose their will, succeeded in alienating all but the remaining Catholic families and clans that had held fast against the storm of the Reformation. Inevitably, he went one step too far. Charles's attempt to introduce the Anglican Liturgy into the Scottish Kirk service sparked a determined rebellion against his authority that quickly fanned the flames of both religious and political discontent on both sides of the border.

It began with the drafting of the Scottish National Covenant, in which all signatories pledged on the one hand their loyalty to their king and, on the other to uphold the 'true faith' of the Kirk of Scotland while, in vitriolic terms, affirming also their undying contempt for the Catholic Church:

> … We abhor and detest all contrary religion and doctrine, but chiefly all kind of papistry … we detest and refuse the usurped authority of that Roman Antichrist upon the Scriptures of God … his corrupted doctrine

concerning original sin, our natural inability and rebellion to God's law, our justification by faith only, our imperfect sanctification and obedience to the law, the nature, number, and use of the holy sacraments; his five bastard sacraments, with all his rites, ceremonies, and false doctrine, added to the ministration of the true sacraments, without the Word of God; his cruel judgements against infants departing without the sacrament; his absolute necessity of baptism; his blasphemous opinion of transubstantiation or real presence of Christ's body in the elements, and receiving of the same by the wicked, or bodies of men; his dispensations, with solemn oaths, perjuries, and degrees of marriage forbidden in the Word; his cruelty against the innocent divorced; his devilish mass; his blasphemous priesthood; his profane sacrifice for the sins of the dead and the quick; his canonization of men, his calling upon angels or saints departed, worshipping of imagery, relics, and crosses; his dedicating of kirks, altars, days, vows to creatures; his purgatory, prayers for the dead, praying or speaking in a strange language; his processions and blasphemous litany, and multitude of advocates or mediators; his manifold orders, auricular confession; his desperate and uncertain repentance; his general and doubtsome faith; his satisfactions of men for their sins; his justification by works, opus operatum, works of supererogation, merits, pardons, peregrinations and stations; his holy water, baptizing of bells, conjuring of spirits, crossing, saning, anointing, conjuring ...

At this point, reading between the lines, Charles I might have sensed that there lay a certain strength of feeling behind this document. It took a death wish of monumental proportions to decide now to start beating this wasps' nest with a stick. Charles decided to assert his authority. Always short of money, he eventually cobbled an army together. The Covenanters massed their forces and by 1639 the two sides were squaring up to each other. Most of the action took place not between the Scots and the English but between the Scottish Royalists and the Scottish Covenanters. The first Bishops' War, as it was called, ended in a climb-down for Charles but, now all the more determined to put the Covenanters in their place, he decided to recall Parliament in the hope of being granted funds to fight the Scots from a position of military strength. As a monarch who had for eleven years sustained an autocratic reign without a single session of Parliament, he might have expected that they had other issues that they wanted to discuss before getting around to voting on funds for another attack on the Scots. The 'Short Parliament' lasted three weeks. For a second time, Charles had to go it alone but this time the Scots did not wait to be attacked; they invaded England. Charles was again forced to sue for peace. Negotiations were scheduled but in the meantime the Scots had no plans to return home. Until the matter was settled, they were going to remain in the north of England and Charles would have to pay their expenses. He was forced to recall Parliament again. The 'Long Parliament' met on 3 November 1640, and the rest, as they say, is history.

It had been like a particularly bad game of chess. Having completely misread the Scottish gambit, Charles was a lot more than a bishop down, he had effectively placed himself in the hands of his English enemies. He had to pay the Scots compensation of £300,000. The English Parliament now set about systematically demolishing his power base. They impeached his two closest advisors, Archbishop Laud and the Earl of Strafford; they abolished the dreaded Star Chamber, and cut off Charles's main sources of independent income, while consolidating and building upon their own power. On 22 November 1641, they voted on the Grand Remonstrance, the famous catalogue of complaints against Charles's policies which, like the National Covenant, ostensibly imputed no blame on the part of the King for the folly and evil ambitions of his secretly pro-Catholic advisors.

In the ensuing Civil War, the Scots Covenanters eventually joined forces with the Parliamentarians. September 1643 saw the signing of the Solemn League and Covenant, another wonderfully constructed document which essentially formalised the Scots alliance with the King's enemies to wage war on the King's forces, for the purpose of removing all trace of Catholicism, and all this, ostensibly, in defence of the King:

> We shall ... without respect of persons, endeavour the extirpation of
> Popery, prelacy, superstition, heresy, schism, profaneness ... endeavour

with our estates and lives mutually to preserve the rights and privileges of the Parliaments, and the liberties of the kingdoms, and to preserve and defend the King's Majesty's person and authority, in the preservation and defence of the true religion ...

The Scots also believed that this document guaranteed the establishment of the Presbyterian system in England but they were rather hoist by their own petard in this respect. The wording was ambiguous. It called for 'the reformation of religion in the kingdoms of England and Ireland, in doctrine, worship, discipline and government, according to the Word of God, and the example of the best reformed Churches', but the Covenanters were so used to interpreting the Word of God in their own way and denying, absolutely, the validity of any other interpretation, that the ambiguity passed unnoticed.

In the early part of the war, the Scottish army did help turn the tide in favour of the Parliamentarians, and their support of Cromwell's Ironsides at Marston Moor, in particular, was instrumental in ending Royalist power in the north of England. By the following year, the King's forces were on the back foot and the New Model Army was proving itself at Naseby. The Royalists never recovered from that defeat. In May 1646, rather than put himself at the mercy of the Parliamentarians, Charles surrendered to the Scots – yet another miscalculation; a few months later, they handed him over to the English and returned home. It was 30 January 1647. Charles had exactly two years to live. For some time, he was kept under a very low-security house arrest at Hampton Court Palace. Discussions with Cromwell took place in these relaxed surroundings. Discussions with the Scots were also being conducted, but covertly via the Earl of Lauderdale, and these seemed to offer more hope of a way out. Some of the Scots were now talking about siding with the King if he could promise to establish the Presbytery in England. Provided they had their way concerning religion, the King could have his way in all other matters.

Now that the common enemy was defeated, the full extent of the differences between the political and religious factions among the

Parliamentarians was exposed, each having felt that the obstacle to achieving their goal had been removed. There was a great deal of heat and not much light. Amid rumours of a possible assassination, Charles escaped or rather walked out unobserved from Hampton Court. He got as far as Carisbrook Castle on the Isle of Wight where he ultimately found himself to be a prisoner in a more strict sense than he had ever been at Hampton Court. Discussions with the Scots, meanwhile – the Lords Loudon, Lauderdale and Lanark – were continued there and, unfortunately, they made some progress.

At Parliament, these Scots commissioners had been openly disagreeing with the English as to what was to be demanded of the King. The consequences of their having overlooked the ambiguity in the Solemn League and Covenant were now evident, whether they saw it in these terms or not. The establishment of the Presbytery that had been central to their support of the Parliamentary cause was now looking more and more unlikely. They felt marginalised and betrayed. The secret negotiations at Carisbrook finally produced a formal agreement, 'The Engagement':

> His Majesty giving belief to the professions of those who have entered into the League and Covenant, and that their intentions are real for preservation of His Majesty's person and authority according to their allegiance, and no ways to diminish his just power and greatness, His Majesty, so soon as he can with freedom, honour and safety be present in a free Parliament, is content to confirm the said League and Covenant by Act of Parliament in both kingdoms, for security of all who have taken or shall take the said Covenant, provided that none who is unwilling shall be constrained to take it. His Majesty will likewise confirm by Act of Parliament in England, Presbyterial government, the Directory for Worship, and Assembly of Divines at Westminster for three years, so that His Majesty and his household be not hindered from using that form of Divine Service he hath formerly practiced ...
>
> and, forasmuch as His Majesty is willing to give satisfaction concerning the settling of religion and other matter in difference, as is expressed in

this Agreement, the kingdom of Scotland doth oblige and engage themselves, first in a peaceable way and manner, to endeavour that His Majesty may come to London in safety, honour and freedom for a personal treaty with the Houses of Parliament and the Commissioners of Scotland upon such Propositions as shall be mutually agreed on between the kingdoms, and such Propositions as His Majesty shall think fit to make; and that, for this end, all armies may be disbanded;

And in case this shall not be granted, that Declarations shall be emitted by the kingdom of Scotland in pursuance of this Agreement, against the unjust proceedings of the two Houses of Parliament towards His Majesty and the kingdom of Scotland, wherein they shall assert the right which belongs to the Crown in the power of the militia, the Great Seal, bestowing of honours and offices of trust, choice of Privy Councillors, the light of the King's negative voice in Parliament; and that the Queen's Majesty, the Prince, and the rest of the royal issue, ought to remain where His Majesty shall think fit, in either of the kingdoms, with safety, honour and freedom;

And upon the issuing of the said Declarations, that an army shall be sent from Scotland into England, for preservation and establishment of religion, for defence of His Majesty's person and authority, and restoring him to his government, to the just rights of the Crown and his full revenues ...

His Majesty or any by his authority or knowledge shall not make nor admit of any cessation, pacification, nor agreement for peace whatsoever, nor of any Treaty, Propositions, Bills, or any other ways for that end, with the Houses of Parliament or any army or party in England and Ireland, without the advice and consent of the kingdom of Scotland ...

His Majesty shall contribute his utmost endeavours both at home and abroad for assisting the kingdom of Scotland in carrying on this war by sea and land, and for their supply by monies, arms, ammunition, and all other things requisite, as also for guarding the coasts of Scotland with ships, and protecting all Scottish merchants in the free exercise of trade and commerce with other nations; and His Majesty is very willing and doth authorize the Scots army to possess themselves of Berwick, Carlisle,

Newcastle-upon-Tyne, Tynemouth, and Hartlepool, for to be places of retreat and magazine …

So, for a second time, there was to be war and once again the Scots were to fight on English soil but this time they would be fighting on the King's side, puritan against puritan. The Royalist revolt started irregularly with pockets of rebellion springing up here and there, many of which had been dealt with by the time the Scots arrived on the scene. Crucially, the 'Engagement' did not have anything like universal support in Scotland. The more extreme Covenanters, the foremost being the power-conscious Marquis of Argyll, Archibald Campbell, were far from ready to side with their malignant King. In the field, the Scottish army, such as it was, proved to be no match for Cromwell when they met at Preston in August. They surrendered shortly after that defeat, followed by the last outposts of Royalist support.

It was doubly disastrous for Scotland. The moderate 'Engagers' were removed from office and the power shifted to Argyll and the ultra-religious Kirk Party, fundamentalist Covenanters led by Argyll's friend, advocate Archibald Johnston of Warriston. Along with Kirk leader Alexander Henderson, Johnston of Warriston had been responsible for the drafting of the National Covenant. He was reputed to have been in the habit of praying for up to five hours a day. He once explained that he had no doubt at all that when his time came he would go to Heaven, having communicated so directly with the Almighty throughout his life and having, more than once during prayer, seen the face of God. It was said that a dinner grace once lasted a full hour and that on another occasion his wife, who had been standing at his side during one of his lengthy prayers, eventually fainted. Johnston carried on praying, regardless. Argyll, Johnston of Warriston and the Kirk Party were now in a position to exercise their puritanical authority to glorify God without restraint of an opposing voice. The Act of Classes was passed, banning from public office all Royalists and Engagers, the duration of the ban depending upon the degree of their involvement in the Engagement. Some were banned for life.

The English Parliament blamed Charles, personally, for this second wave of unnecessary bloodshed. He was tried and found guilty of treason. His execution, however, united Scotland against the new republic. The following week, the Scottish Parliament declared his exiled nineteen-year-old son Charles II, King of Scotland, England, France and Ireland. As might be expected, there were conditions: he had to accept the Covenants. Inevitably, there were negotiations, and while the negotiations were ongoing, Charles II, very much his father's son, was planning an alternative to the consultative process.

James Graham, Marquis of Montrose had achieved legendary status in his military support for Charles I. While most of Scotland was siding with the Parliamentarians, Montrose had been waging a seemingly unstoppable Royalist campaign in Scotland. He was a Covenanter and a Royalist when every Scot who was willing to put his head above the parapet was either one or the other. His support for Charles I arose, arguably, out of loyalty not only to his King but also to his country. The thought of the King being defeated and Scotland being effectively left in the control of Argyll had spurred him to acts of heroism and military brilliance that carried his name across Europe. Charles II now thought he could make use of this Royalist folk hero who had served so well as his father's lieutenant in Scotland. He re-appointed Montrose, now on the Continent, as Lieutenant Governor and Captain General of Scotland and privately authorised him to take over the country by force.

Montrose's plan to enter Scotland via Orkney with troops that he had enlisted on the Continent was utterly hopeless, primarily because unlike his earlier campaigns, which had gathered momentum naturally, this attempted uprising was arranged remotely and with either astonishingly unreliable or deliberately misleading intelligence of the real situation in Scotland. Having been led to believe he would have the support of the northern clans, he was effectively lured into completely hostile territory. Two of the very clans that Montrose expected to join him were indeed waiting for him but only to join the attack on his mainly German and Danish troops. The ensuing battle of Carbisdale caught him completely off-guard and his foreign soldiers were being pursued and massacred for several days after. Montrose himself was soon captured and taken to Edinburgh for trial.

Charles II, meanwhile, had been hedging his bets. He had continued negotiations with the Covenanters and shortly after Montrose's defeat, in signing the Treaty of Breda on 1 May 1650, Charles conceded without qualification everything that he and his father had stubbornly rejected. He also disowned Montrose's commission, paving the way for Argyll, three weeks later, to avenge former military defeat and witness Montrose's execution. On 23 June, at the mouth of the River Spey, before setting foot in Scotland, Charles signed to both of the Covenants. He was a king, in the power of a Scottish Parliament, in the power of Argyll and the Kirk Party. His contempt for his pious masters must have multiplied with every interminable sermon he was forced to endure as a proof of his sincerity and devotion to the 'true faith.' As further evidence of that sincerity, the removal of all 'malignants' from the King's counsel was now requested. No one who had access to the King should be of a doubtful stance with respect to their wholehearted allegiance to the Covenant.

27 June 1650

The committee appointed for conference with the commissioners from the church thought it appropriate that some persons should be sent to congratulate his Majesty's happy arrival into this kingdom and to show his Majesty how glad his people were to hear that it has pleased God to move his heart to give satisfaction to their desires, and that it would be very acceptable to them that, to testify his reality therein, he would likewise forsake and abandon the company of malignants and that his domestic servants, and such as are about him, might be well affected to the cause and not malignant, and such as are otherwise, be removed and put from about him, but in a fair and discreet way.

And having considered the list of his Majesty's servants and others of the train, so far as it comes to their knowledge, the committee aforesaid thought it fit and necessary that the persons afterfollowing, viz., The Duke of Hamilton, the Duke of Buckingham, the Earl Forth, Lauderdale, Sir Robert Dalzell, Lt. Sinclair, Doctor Frazer, Lt. Wilmott, Lt. Wentworth, Secretary Long, Mr Uder, Earl of Cleveland, Mr Seymor, Viscount Grandison, Mr Progers, Lt. Withrington, Mr Rogers, Sir Philip Musgrave, Col. Darcy, Col. Gray, Col. Boynton, Major Jackson, Dr Goff, Mr Harding, corrupt chaplaines, and Sir Edward Walker, should forthwith remove themselves and depart out of the kingdom; and such also as have served in arms against the cause, and been evil instruments and given bad counsel to his Majesty's late father and himself, and likewise such others as upon information from our Commissioners, shall be thought fit to be removed.

Meanwhile Cromwell had mobilised against Scotland. On 22 July, his army crossed the Tweed and a few days later they were outside Edinburgh and with a fleet of fifteen ships lying off the coast with supplies. Some accounts tell that up to 40,000 Scottish soldiers had gathered on the Links at Leith to make ready for war. But this was to be war in the name of God. Volunteers had come from all over Scotland to put their lives on the line for their King and country, but that was not good enough for the Church; they first had to be tested as to their loyalty to the 'true' religion. The cause of fighting for the King had attracted a great number of the wrong sort of people, with varying degrees of malignancy, even secret Catholics. Association with such people could only be expected to bring the wrath of God down upon them all. Accordingly, every man found to be lacking true Protestant zeal was sent home. They almost halved the army.

The King's chronicler, Sir Edward Walker (Secretary of War to Charles I, and Clerk to the Council of Charles II), makes no effort to disguise his bewilderment at this drastic reduction of fighting strength:

By this time, Cromwell was entered Scotland and, without any opposition, had advanced to Mussleburgh, but six miles from Edinburgh. The
Scottish Army was drawn between Leith and Edinburgh, having cast a
trench before them. The number, at that time, of either army were equal,

each being about 12,000 men but Cromwell's, at that time, in much better order and discipline, for the Scottish army, being solely governed by
the Committee of Estates [the Scottish Parliament] and the Kirk, took
especial care in the recruitment not to admit any Malignants or Engagers,
placing, for the most part, in command, ministers' sons, clerks, and such
other sanctified creatures who hardly ever saw or heard of any sword but
that of the Spirit, and with this, their chosen crew, made themselves sure
of victory.

There was, of course, one notorious malignant who couldn't be sent
home: the King, himself. Wherever he went, his effect on the army was
to raise morale. Even this was alarming to the Kirk. Many of the men
now chalked a crown over an R on their arms to show how they felt
about having their King with them. This was absolutely unacceptable.
The King had to be persuaded to keep away from the troops. The common soldiers were obviously becoming confused as to what they were
fighting for.

In August, in a further attempt to bring God onside, the King was
asked to put his name to a declaration distancing himself from all forms
of malignancy, including his own parents:

Though his Majesty, as a dutiful son, be obliged to honour the memory
of his royal father, and to have in estimation the person of his mother yet
doth he desire to be deeply humbled and afflicted in spirit before God,
because of his father's opposition to the work of God, and to the solemn
league and covenant, by which so much of the blood of the Lord's people
hath been shed in these kingdoms; and for the idolatry of his mother,
the toleration whereof in the kings house, as it was a matter of grate
humbling to all the Protestant churches, so could it not be but a high
provocation against him, who is a jealous God, visiting the sins of the
fathers upon the children ...

It was not enough. Cromwell, to his own surprise, was eventually to get
the better of the Scottish army. Up until now, he had been able to thole

any setbacks, confident in the knowledge that God would know he had tried, always, to do the right thing. He had been untroubled about the death toll in Ireland, said to have approached 618,000, two-fifths of the entire population. The previous year's mass murder of Irish Catholics in Drogheda had, in Cromwell's eyes, been work to glorify God but this war with the Calvinist Scots was a different thing entirely. Cromwell had always had some misgivings about attacking his puritan neighbours. By the end of August, his lack of success was undermining his confidence that he had the Almighty's approval. He offered to parley with the Scots asking only to be allowed to return to England unmolested. This, however, only convinced the Committee of Estates and the Kirk that it was they who had the Lord's blessing.

Cromwell was followed to Dunbar where, as he began transferring the wounded to the waiting ships, he now found himself trapped. In spite of the efforts of the Kirk the Scottish army now vastly outnumbered Cromwell's forces. Lt General David Leslie placed his men in a commanding position on a hill overlooking the English. While the options were being discussed, the Kirk leaders took the opportunity to weed out some more malignants from the army. It is said they sent away up to 3,000 men over a three-day period.

Leslie's instincts were to let Cromwell pass on terms but his saintly masters wanted blood; he was ordered to attack. As night fell on 2 September, he brought his men down from the hill in preparation for an assault the following morning. Cromwell watched in disbelief. Under cover of darkness and a raging storm, he moved his men into position for a pre-emptive strike in the first faint light of dawn. About half of the Scots army escaped the carnage with their lives. They regrouped at Stirling and awaited Cromwell's next attack. It was to be a long wait; Cromwell was content to consolidate. Before the end of the year, lowland Scotland would effectively be in his power.

The Committee of Estates still met and the extremists in the Kirk still blamed malignancy for bringing God's wrath upon the nation. Those of Charles's malignant advisors who had managed to remain, in defiance of the original order for them to leave the country, were removed from his presence. Offers of help from nobles and clan chiefs all over the country were still coming in and still being turned down. Charles, however, had seen enough. On Friday, 4 October, dressed in thin riding clothes as if he was going hawking, he left Perth on horseback along with a few servants. He rode casually until he was well out of the area then, at a gallop, he headed north. He met with Viscount Dudhope at Dundee and then the earl of Buchan. They rode with him to Cortoquhy Castle, the seat of James Ogilvy, Earl of Airlie who was one of the leading Catholic nobles, a long-standing enemy of Argyll, and one who had fought alongside Montrose. After Cortoquhy, he rode on, now accompanied by a guard of eighty highland men, and he spent the night in a small cottage owned by Ogilvy of Clova. It all looked very promising but before morning his keepers' men, soon accompanied by 600 horses, had caught up with him. They found him lying in 'a nastie room on an auld bolster on a mat of rushes, over-wearied and very fearful.' They had him back in Perth by Sunday.

With or without the company of their King, the northern clans were determined to fight but even now the Estates and the Kirk not only rejected them but sent troops to oppose them. The cries for unity fell on deaf ears.

26 October 1650

The Northern Band and Oath of Engagement, sent by Middleton to Lt. General David Leslie: We, the underscribers, being touched with a deep sense of the sad condition this our native Kingdom of Scotland is in, by a prevailing army of sectarians, who having murdered our late King, and overturned religion and government in our neighbour kingdoms of England and Ireland, hath invaded this Kingdom, and, having so considerable a part of it underfoot already, are about to reduce the whole to a province, unless the Lord by his mercy prevent it by joining his Majesty's subjects in a band of unity, which is the only means (in our judgement) to preserve religion, king and kingdoms. But, to the grief of our hearts, we find, in place of union, the breach growing wider, and that not only in church and state, but likewise, in the remnant of our army. Our resolutions are firmly and faithfully to join ourselves together, and neither for fear, threatening, allurement, nor advantage, to relinquish so good a cause or to lay down arms, without a general consent; and what shall be done to the least of us, in prosecuting the said union, shall be taken as done to us all. And seeing the best undertakings are under the mercy of censure and malice, we cannot but apprehend to be subject to the lawless inquisition. Therefor, and for satisfaction to all who are satisfiable, we do promise and swear that we shall maintain the true religion, as it is established in Scotland, the Covenant, the League and Covenant, the King's Majesty's person, prerogative, greatness and authority, the privileges of Parliament and freedom of the subjects. So help us God.

Sic subscribitur: Huntly, Athole, Seafort, St Clare, Jo. Middleton, Pat. Graham, Sir Geo. Munro, Th. MacKenzie, Jo. Gordon, Wanderrosse, W. Horrie.

The records of the Scots Parliament show that on the evening of 5 December, the King being present, the Scottish Regalia (i.e. the Crown, the Sceptre and the Sword of State), were lying in their splendour, adorning a table beside the throne. Candles were lit in the house, and to general surprise, a 'great stock owl' flew in and 'muttit' [left its droppings] on the top of the crown. Opinion will be divided as to whether the wisdom often attributed to this particular bird had, for the moment, deserted it or was merely further evidenced on this occasion.

By the end of 1650, the Scots were split in two clear factions: the Resolutioners who, supporting the resolutions expressed by Middleton, sought unity and argued that all Scots, whether Covenanter or Royalist, should be allowed to defend their country; and the Remonstrants, the religious extremists who were all the more convinced that Charles and his malignant followers should be completely disowned. The more moderate Resolutioners, however, were now in much greater number and winning the argument. Power was gradually shifting into their hands. Royalists and 'Engagers' were, once again, being permitted to join the army. At Scone on 1 January 1651, Argyll performed his last act as a major player by placing the crown on Charles II's head. By June, the Royalists had recovered sufficient power to repeal the Act of Classes that had banned so many of their number from office.

It was July 1651 before Cromwell moved to probe for weaknesses in the King's army at Stirling. Finding them well prepared for a direct assault, he pulled back to Edinburgh and, against expectations, transported his army across the River Forth at Queensferry. The news threw the Scots into some confusion; all their defences had been organised to repel an attack from south of the river. Charles made a decision which, had it worked, would have been hailed as a masterstroke. On 31 July, he led his army south into England, hoping to draw the English Royalists and perhaps even Presbyterians to his flag.

The Scots were about to pay the penalty for putting their King in charge of the army. This was not strategy; it was wishful thinking. Leslie had been urging Charles to stay in Scotland, to deal with Cromwell in familiar territory and with known resources. History proved him right. The English, as might be expected, were not slow to take measures to discourage and limit any potential Royalist attempts to join the Scots. Cromwell's forces outnumbered them by two to one when they finally met at Worcester on 3 September. The date, incidentally, was exactly two years after Cromwell's victory at Dunbar and seven years before his death on 3 September 1658. Following the Scots' total defeat at Worcester, Charles, having narrowly escaped with his life, eventually managed to flee the country and spent the next nine years as an exile on the Continent, during which time he made himself as useful as might any monarch, sans people, sans kingdom, sans crown.

Chapter Two

Just south of Stonehaven, on the north-east coast of Scotland, Dunnottar Castle towers in dramatic isolation, 160ft above sea level, on a craggy, almost perpendicular rock. On one side, it is pounded by the relentless ferocity of the North Sea and, on the other, it is virtually separated from the mainland by a deep natural chasm. The only approach begins with a descent into this valley which renders any would-be assailants completely at the mercy of the castle battlements. Having crossed the open valley, they would come to a narrow path which winds steeply around the rock and leads, finally, to a portcullis at the base of a 40ft wall. Behind this, a tunnel leads on up a further incline, terminating with an array of loop-holes bristling with muskets.

This was the seat of William Keith, Earl Marschall of Scotland. His ancestors had created for themselves not only a formidable fortress but a splendid, almost palatial dwelling. Behind the battlements on the plateau top of this rock, the grass-covered expanse (of which, over the centuries, very few uninvited guests had ever seen), were the barracks, lodgings, stables, stores, armoury, keep, banqueting hall, and a chapel, eleven buildings in all. The domestic apartments were well appointed, literally fit for a king. The Marschall was, traditionally, the king's lieutenant in Scotland and the Keiths had held that hereditary duty and honour since the end of the twelfth century. Sir Robert Keith had led the Scots cavalry at Bannockburn and since then the family had continued to grow in power and distinction. They were, at one point, the wealthiest family in Scotland and it is still remembered that in those days the Earl Marschall could ride from Berwick to Caithness and stay on his own property every night.

In June 1651, while Cromwell occupied Edinburgh and the Scottish army prepared for his expected assault on Stirling, the Committee of Estates made provision for the safety of, amongst other things, the Scottish Regalia – the Honours of Scotland: the Crown, Sceptre and Sword – by placing them in the custody of the Earl Marschall. Cromwell had already destroyed the English Crown Jewels. The Regalia were locked away in Dunnottar and a garrison was established there under the command of Capt. George Ogilvy of Barrass.

Commission – the Earl Marschall to George Ogilvy of Barras.

> Forasmuch as the King's Majesty and Committee of Estates have entrusted the care of the keeping of the house and castle of Dunnottar to us William Earl Marschall, and have allowed forty men, a lieutenant and two servants to be entertained within it upon the public charge, therefore, we do hereby nominate George Ogilvy of Barrass to be our lieutenant for keeping of the said house, and give unto him the sole and full power of the Command thereof and of the men that are to be entertained therein for keeping thereof, under us, with power to him to bruik, enjoy and exercise the said place with all the fees, dues and allowances belonging thereto, as fully in all respects as any other lieutenant in such a case may do. In witness whereof we have subscribed these presents at Stirling, the 8 of July 1651. – Marschall.
>
> Witnesses: W Keith, A Lindesay, A Primerose

On returning south to finish off the Royalist army, Cromwell had left Lt General George Monck with the job of mopping up the remaining pockets of resistance in Scotland. Receiving intelligence that the Committee of Estates were meeting at Alyth, near Kirriemuir in Angus, Monck sent a party to apprehend them. In a surprise attack on 28 August, one of those captured on the way to the meeting was William Keith, the Earl Marschall.

Before he and the other prisoners were shipped off to London and the Tower, he succeeded in negotiating the release of his uncle, Robert Keith of Whiteriggs, presumably on the grounds of his being a non-combatant. The Earl Marschall now entrusted to his uncle the key to the strongroom containing the Regalia, together with a message to be taken to the Earl Marschall's mother, the Dowager Countess, Marie Erskine, asking her to go with Whiteriggs to Dunnottar and to see to the safety of these last symbols of Scotland's independence.

The Earl Marschall may have hoped that the Regalia could be hidden somewhere on his mother's property at Bolshan, south of Brechin. By the time she went to Dunnottar, however, the English troops had reached nearby Stonehaven. The castle was not yet under siege but, nevertheless, the Countess would have been conscious of the risk involved in attempting to remove the Regalia. In the event, she handed the key to Ogilvy and told him, more or less: 'you're the Governor of the castle; you take care of it.'

Meanwhile, the Committee of Estates had written to Ogilvy:

Aberdeen – 31 August 1651.
For George Ogilvy Deputy Governor of the Castle of Dunnottar.

> Loving friend, – It being thought fit that the honours of the Crown should be, for their further security, removed from the castle, the Laird of Innes was sent on Saturday last to receive them but, on account of your absence, nothing was done. We have again sent these to you to know your resolution that accordingly we may send someone to receive them. Whatever falls out of this, it will be an exoneration to us. You shall also send to us an account of the condition of the house of Dunnottar, what you hear of the enemy's motions, and of the resolutions of the Shire of Kincardine ... We are, Your assured friends, – Calander, A.G. Durie, Sir Th. Nicolson, Sir J Innes, A. Belsches, Rbt. Farquar.

George Ogilvy was in a difficult position. If he hands over the Regalia, and they subsequently fall into the hands of the enemy, the responsibility would be his: 'we have again sent these to you to know your resolution'. The Estates, reluctant to explicitly order the removal of the Regalia, now write to Alexander Lindsay, Earl of Balcarres, in the hope of bringing some authority to bear upon Ogilvy:

10 Sept 1651

Right Honourable, – the Committee of Estates taking into their consideration how necessary it is, in this time of trouble, that special care be
taken of the safe custody of the Honours of the Crown and the King's
stuff which were sent to Dunnottar, we desire your Lordship that you
would take a speedy and effectual way for the preservation thereof, where
they may be surest kept from danger which, trusting your Lordship will
carefully perform, we rest, Your Lordship's very affectionate friends, –
Wigton; Loudon, Chancellor; Lothian; Argyll; Sir James Wemis Bogie;
Linlithgow; Sir Arthur Stirling; Home; Blair of Ard Blair; Wemis; James
Manteith; Mr Geo. Dundass; Mr John Cowen.

Once again, a definitive instruction as to what precisely was to be done,
and by whose authority, was absent. Balcarres visited Dunnottar and
tried to persuade Ogilvy of the inevitable consequences of keeping the
Regalia in the castle but he was no more successful. In October, he
writes to Ogilvy:

Sir, – you are now, I believe, hardly in expectation of relief and you know
how much it concerns not only the kingdom but yourself in particular
that the Honours be secured. I shall, therefore, again desire you, by virtue
of the first warrant which you saw and of this, likewise, which I have
lately received and now send you enclosed, that you deliver them immediately after the receipt hereof to the bearer, Sir Arthur Forbes, whose
receipt of them, under his hand, I do hereby declare shall be as valid for
your acquittal and liberation as if you had it under the hand of, Your
affectionate friend to serve you, – Balcarres. – I shall not now repeat the
arguments I used to you at Dunnottar. If they were strong then, I am sure
they are much more now, for the circumstances are much altered since. I
say no more but remember what I then spoke to you as your friend.

Replying to Balcarres, (ibid. Preface) Ogilvy points out that, still, no spe-
cific order has been given either for Balcarres to remove or for himself

to deliver the Regalia. Given enough men, food and ammunition, Ogilvy believed there to be no more secure place in the country than Dunnottar but if the Estates thought otherwise, and provided he got an order from them together with an exoneration to the Earl Marschall and to himself, he was happy to bow to their better judgement. He writes to the chancellor, the Earl of Loudon, in the same strain, complaining that more than half of the food he was promised has been sold off elsewhere and asking, also, for another sixty men. (ibid. Supplementary Papers no.2.)

A very civil dialogue now opened between Ogilvy and the occupying forces:

Stane Hive (Stonehaven) – 8 November 1651.
General Overton, for the Honourable Governor of Dunnottar Castle and the rest of the Gentlemen there.

> Gentlemen, – I have power to demolish your own house and the remainder of the Lord Marschall's houses in these parts, unless you timeously prevent the same by giving up the Castle of Dunnottar to the use of the State of England upon such terms as other gentlemen of honour have heretofore accepted (when the forces of this nation were more significant). You may observe that this season closes with the most significant persons of your nation having put their persons and estates under our protection. You may likewise consider how imprudent, or at least improvident a part it may be reputed, in a time of pacification, for yourselves to be the only antagonists to an army whose arms God Almighty has hitherto made successful against your most considerable citadels. I dare not promise you the like opportunity for good terms in future as all is ready at present to be performed upon speedy capitulation. Who rests, gentlemen, Your humble servant, – R. Overton.

Ogilvy, in his reply, makes exactly the right move. He simply bluffs, declaring that the Earl Marschall's property can not be held to ransom since his orders did not come from the Earl Marschall.

Dunnottar, same day, George Ogilvy to General Overton.

Sir, – I have received yours, and, in answer, you shall know that I have my commission absolutely from the King's Majesty and none else, wherefore you may do what you please with my Lord Marschall's houses for he has no interest in this, which, by the help of the Lord, I intend to preserve to the uttermost of my life till I have further orders from His Majesty. And the success you have had in former times shall in no way move me to the contrary, for I know that the Lord is above you to whose providence I entrust myself. And bid you farewell Sir, Your Servant, George Ogilvy.

On 13 November, the Earl of Loudon added his voice to the chorus of concern over the fate of the Regalia:

For my much respected friend, George Ogilvie, Governor of Dunnottar. Sir, – Your letter of the last of October, came to my hand upon the 9th of November … but the Parliament not having met, and there being no meeting of the Committee of Estates, I can give you no positive advice nor order. But I conceive that the trust committed to you, and the safe custody of these things under your charge did require that victual, a competent number of honest and stout soldiers, and all other necessaries, should have been provided and put on the castle before you were in any hazard.

If you can timely supply yourself with all necessaries, and if the place be tenable against all attempts of the enemy, I do not doubt that you will hold out. But if you want provisions, soldiers and ammunition, and cannot hold out at the assaults of the enemy, which it is feared and thought you cannot do; if you be hard pursued, I know no better expedient, than that the Honours of the Crown, be speedily and safely transported to some remote and strong castle or hold in the highlands.

And I wish you had delivered them to the Lord Balcarras, as was desired by the Committee of Estates, nor do I know any better way, for the preservation of these things, and your exoneration. And it will be an irreparable loss and shame, if these things shall be taken by the enemy,

and very dishonourable for yourself. I have herewith returned your letter to Lord Balcarras, hearing he is still in the north. I have written to
Sir John Smyth to furnish to you the remainder of the provisions you
say he should have given you. So, having given you the best advice I can
at present, I trust you will, with all care and faithfulness, be answerable
according to the trust committed to you, and I shall still remain, Your
very assured & real friend, – Loudoun, Cancellarius.

Stone Hyve – 22 November 1651.
Colonel Dutton, for the Commander in Chief of Dunnottar Castle.

Honoured Sir – Whereas you keep Dunnottar Castle for the use of your
King; which castle does belong to the Lord Marschall, who is now prisoner to our Parliament of England. These are to advise and require you,
in their names, to surrender the said castle to me, for their use. And I do
assure you, by the word of a gentleman, that you shall have very honourable and soldier-like conditions. If you refuse this offer then, if any thing
shall happen to you contrary to your expectations by the violence of our
soldiers, blame yourself and not me; for I may tell you that the Lord has
been pleased, to deliver unto us many stronger places by storm since our
unhappy difference has been. And I doubt not but the same God will
stand by us, in our attempts in this. I desire your speedy answer, and shall
rest, Sir, your very humble servant, Tho. Dutton.

Dunnottar, same day, Ogilvy to Colonel Dutton.

Honoured Sir, – Whereas you write that I keep the Castle of Dunnottar
for the use of the King's Majesty which house (as you say) belongs to the
Earl Marschall; you shall know I have my commission absolutely from his
Majesty and none else, neither will I acknowledge any man's interest here,
and I intend, by the assistance of God, to maintain the same for his Majesty's
service upon all hazard whatsoever. I hope you have that much gallantry in
you, as not to wrong my Lord Marschall's lands, seeing he is a prisoner
himself and has no relation to this place for the present. Whereas you have

had success in former times, I attribute it to the wrath of God against us and the unfaithfulness of those men who did maintain the same, none whereof you shall find here, by the Lord's Grace, to whom I commit myself, and am, Sir, Your very humble servant, – George Ogilvy.

The Cromwellians could afford to be patient; Ogilvy was not doing them any harm and he certainly was not going anywhere. In many respects, the English were finding their relationship with the Scots much less confrontational than they might have expected. After years of what was, essentially, rule by the Kirk, it would have to be a fairly brutal regime not to be an improvement. An excerpt from Chambers' *Domestic Annals of Scotland* gives an example of this other side to the coin of the English occupation:

At this time, a lively controversy was going on between Sir Alexander Irvine of Drum and the Presbytery of Aberdeen, as to their assumed right to control his spiritual interests. A quarrel had arisen over the choice of incumbent in Sir Alexander's parish, and he had appealed from the power of the local court to the English commander, Colonel Overton – a proceeding which must have been deeply grievous to the Presbytery. A sentence of excommunication having been pronounced against the knight, he protested against it in animated terms. It proceeded, he said, 'from men more full of fiery zeal to advance their own interests than the gospel of Jesus Christ.' They had urged him, by threats, to subscribe the Solemn League and Covenant, 'as if it was a matter of salvation for me to swear to establish, by arms, Presbyterian government in England.' And not only would they have had him perjure himself, but 'they urged, with like threatening, my wife and my three young daughters who, for their age and sex, are not capable of such politic theology.' To further their charge against him of being a papist – 'a pretext to satisfy their restless ambition and execute their rage upon all who will not implicitly obey them' – they 'forced my servants to reveal, upon oath, what they saw, heard, or knew done in my house – beyond which no Turkish inquisition could pass.' Sir Alexander, therefore, now appeared by procurator, declaring, 'I separate myself from the discipline of Presbytery, particularly that of Aberdeen, as a human invention that is destructive to the civil peace of Christians.'

In Edinburgh, the Commonwealth-appointed English judges were imposing a form of justice that was utterly alien to Scotland at that time. They listened, weighed up the evidence and pronounced their judgements with an impartiality and objectivity that, to their predecessors, was a sore affliction to behold. Some years later, having commented on this aberration to an old Scots judge, a young lawyer was told: 'Devil take them! They had neither kith nor kin in this country. Take that out of the way and I think I could make a good judge myself.'

Cromwell's Commissioners for Justice in Edinburgh, the judges who had taken over the Court of Session, were, on occasion, left in no doubt that it was the prosecutors themselves that should be brought to trial. In the normal course of business, two accused of witchcraft appeared before the Court. They had been brought before the Kirk some months previously. The Court had the unprecedented curiosity to ask how they came to confess to a crime that was punishable by burning at the stake. The witches explained that they had first had their thumbs tied behind them and then, being hung by the thumbs, they had been whipped. This having failed to bring a confession, lighted candles were applied to the soles of their feet and between their toes, and then to the insides their mouths. It transpired that the two who stood before the court had then confessed but that there had originally been six accused, four of whom had died during questioning.

In February 1652, Ogilvy wrote to Charles II telling him, essentially, that Dunnottar was still holding out but it was now the last fortress in the kingdom flying the Royal standard, that the Regalia and other items of the King's property were safe for the present. He explained that the castle was now under siege, only the seaward side being open, and asked for the King's instructions and for any help that might be sent by sea. This was written on 1 February and it seems it reached the King at Paris as late as 11 April. Food was now running short but the occasional commando-style sortie by sea helped them restock from occupied Stonehaven and Aberdeen. Following one of these raids, Ogilvy received a communication from Cromwell's Commissary General, General Walley:

Aberdeen – 10 February 1652.

Sir, – I have received a letter from two of my soldiers, Wm Waddington and Richard Parsons, who give notice that they are prisoners with you. I also heard of two soldiers of yours, prisoners with us at Aberdeen. I have set them at liberty upon parole to come to you, in whose place I expect those two soldiers of mine to return to me with their horses and arms, otherwise I desire you to send those back. If you please to release the third man taken with them, we shall not be behind hand with you in courtesy when time serves. I have no more but to let you know that, wherein I may, I shall be, Your humble servant, E. Walley.

Aberdeen – 15 February 1652.
General Walley to the Governor of the Castle of Dunnottar.

Sir, – If you please to send me my soldiers with their horses and arms, in the end, it will be more to your advantage, than if you send them without. I shall account myself obliged to take care that you may find it so. If you keep the horses, I am content you also keep the men, that they may suffer for being so taken. I have no reason to give my own money out of my purse to redeem their horses, nor have I any other way to do it, except I make your town where they were taken do it, and that they shall do if you desire it, however if the horses be not sent back they must pay their full value. You may, if you please, save the town from a charge and lay an obligation upon one who will be careful to discharge it and in what he may to let you know he is, Your humble servant, E. Walley.

This thoroughly civilised correspondence does not quite paint a complete picture of relations during the pacification of Scotland. Only a few months ago, when Robert Lumsden, the governor of the castle at Dundee had communicated a similar resolve to hold out against Monck, the city was stormed and the inhabitants of the garrison, men and women, young and old, were put to the sword. The rules of war, in those days, sanctioned atrocities on this scale and more, should a town under siege choose to resist rather than capitulate. Upwards of 500 are said to have been massacred subsequent to the surrender and Monck's troops were given licence to rape and pillage for twenty-four hours. There is a footnote to the story: the walled town of Dundee had been considered a safer repository than Edinburgh for the wealth of some of the country's most affluent individuals. Monck, it is alleged, had gathered a fortune in silver, plate and jewellery, together with something in the region of 200,000 gold coins, in the course of his brief visit to Dundee. The whole plunder, known as Monck's Loot, was put aboard ship which, having travelled only a mile or two in the Tay Estuary, foundered on the sandbanks in bad weather. (It was reported in 2002 that an attempt was being made, at a cost of £1,000,000, to find the ship and recover the treasure, reputedly valued at something approaching £2.5 billion.)

It was only a matter of time before the Cromwellians' heavy artillery would be brought up from the south and, from then on, Ogilvy could expect to hold out against a bombardment for a period numbered in days rather than months. His main concern was that the Regalia did not fall into the hands of the English but there were other items of importance that had to be safeguarded. The King's papers were stitched into a belt made by Ogilvy's wife, Elizabeth Douglas, and the documents were thus safely removed from the castle by her niece, Anne Lindsay. The removal of the Regalia, however, would be a much more dangerous affair. When the Countess balked at the idea of carrying off the Honours, Cromwell's troops had been a mile away in Stonehaven. Now they were encamped at Dunnottar itself and in much greater number. Only non-military personnel could apply for a pass to enter and leave the castle.

As a man of the cloth, James Grainger, the minister of Kinneff, was one person who would not be refused access. A graduate of St Andrews University, he was thirty-six years old when, on 6 October 1640, he had become the minister of the tiny Kirk of Kinneff. A few miles south of Dunnottar, it would then have been hard to imagine anywhere more remote from the momentous conflicts and the great affairs of state that troubled the nation at that time. He married twenty-two-year-old Kinneff-born Christian Fletcher and, by 1652, they had two sons: John, aged seven and Robert, aged three.

George Ogilvy was one of the heritors (landowners) of the Parish of Kinneff and, over the years, had had enough business with the minister to know what kind of man he was dealing with. James Grainger was possibly the only man with whom Ogilvy felt free to discuss his predicament. According to Grainger, the governor, by now, was at his wits' end. Grainger offered to help in any way he could and it was finally agreed that he would take charge of the Honours if he could figure a way of getting them out. It was also agreed that from this point onwards, whatever was resolved upon, Ogilvy would not be told any details; the idea being that even if put to torture he could in all honesty swear that he had no knowledge of their whereabouts. The minister and his wife now talked over the whole business and they came up with a plan.

The risk of detection ruled out transporting the Regalia by sea and yet every man leaving Dunnottar by the landward side could expect to be challenged … every man, but not necessarily every woman. It was Grainger's plan but the execution of it fell to the two wives, Elizabeth Douglas and Christian Fletcher. The governor's wife would send a message to the minister's wife, inviting her to come to the castle. A pass was arranged and the two woman had, in Christian Fletcher's own words, 'a little conference.' She then walked out of Dunnottar with the Crown and the Royal Sceptre concealed under her skirts and her winter clothing. During the long descent from the castle, she had ample time to contemplate the possible consequences. As she emerged from the tunnel and followed the path down around the rock and then across the valley, she was now in full view of Cromwell's troops. Her apprehension would increase steadily as she walked toward them, up the steep incline to the English camp where her horse was tethered but her composure did not desert her. It is said that she stopped briefly to chat with some of the guards, and that the Cromwellian Colonel Morgan himself helped her on to her horse. From the moment of leaving the castle, and throughout the 5-mile journey back to Kinneff, she was in fear of her life. She rode back along the cliff tops always keeping near to the sea, resolving, as she later explained, rather to lose her life and throw the Honours into the sea than to let them be taken from her.

That night, when their children were asleep, the Graingers took the Crown and the Sceptre into the church and buried them beneath the flagstones. The following week, James Grainger made another journey to Dunnottar. A way now had to be devised to remove the 4.5ft Sword of State. A few days later, for a second time, Christian Fletcher left Dunnottar, this time on foot and accompanied by her servant. On her servant's back, as far as the girl knew, was a sack containing coarse flax tow and a distaff wrapped in tow ready for spinning. The only hope of avoiding suspicion was for the two young women to walk right through the English camp. The sword, too, was soon safe under the flagstones in the Kinneff church. Still one more journey had to be made for the scabbard. By this time, Chrissie was past caring about the quality of its precious filigree. She folded it over and brought it out concealed inside a sack full of 'cods' (pillows). At the end of March, at Ogilvy's request, Grainger went to the Countess and gave her a full account of what had been done:

> I, Mr James Granger, Minister at Kinneff, grant me to have in my custody, the Honours of the Kingdom of Scotland, viz. the Crown, Sceptre and Sword. For the Crown and Sceptre, I raised a pavement stone just before the pulpit, and dig'd under it a hole and put them in there, and fill'd up the hole and put down the stone just as it was again, and remov'd the Mould that remain'd, that none would have discerned the stone to have been raised at all. The Sword, again, at the west end of the church, among some common seats that stand there, I dig'd down in the ground betwixt the two foremost of the seats, and laid it down within the case of it, and covered it up so that, removing the superfluous mould, it could not be discerned by anybody. And if it shall please God to call me by

death before they be called for, your Ladyship will find them there. Sic Subscribitur, Mr James Granger.

The demands upon Ogilvy to capitulate continued but, the Regalia being secured, he was now in a better position to negotiate terms. Again, Ogilvy made the right move by holding fast for as long as possible:

Dunnottar Castle – 9 May 1652.
George Ogilvy to the Right Honourable Major General Deane Commander in Chief of the English forces in Scotland.

Sir, – In my former letters to General Major Lambert and others about the rendition of this house I was then resolved upon no terms to treat till I should have an absolute warrant from the King's Majesty. But at the earnest desire and persuasion of the Earl Marschall's friends … and for the avoidance of the effusion of blood whereof there has been too much already and, doubtless, with more to follow if not prevented … I thought it fit, hereby, to show you that I am content to go on in the said capitulation … upon honourable terms, and, for that effect shall, give power and warrant to two gentlemen to meet and treat with you at such time as you shall design and make known with this bearer. And if this be not satisfactory to you, you shall find men here, God-willing, ready to wait upon your service, to hazard and lay down their lives before we, in any dishonourable way, betray our trust. And I attest God to be judge between you and us and that he may call for the blood that will be shed at his hands who shall be cause of it so, expecting your answer, and remain, Your servant, George Ogilvy

14 May 1652, The [Cromwellian] camp, Blackhill of Dunnottar –
Colonel Morgan to the Governor of Dunnottar Castle.

Sir, – I am commanded here by the Honourable Major General Deane's order, with a considerable strength of the army, to summon you to surrender the Castle of Dunnottar to me, for the use of the Parliament and the Commonwealth of England, with all the ordnance and other arms, ammunition and provision therein, as also the Crown and Sceptre of Scotland which, doubtless, is in your custody with all ensignia of regality and other goods belonging to the recent king of Scotland. You may take notice of what condition you are in, and so observe this my summons, and prevent that inconvenience which doubtless is like to fall upon you. I shall expect your answer within an hour after the receipt and shall remain at the Blackhill. Your servant, accordingly, – Tho. Morgan

Ogilvy to Colonel Morgan

Sir, – At the desire of my Lord Marschall's special friends whom, next to the King's Majesty, I respect in this business as having the greatest interest here, I have sent my mind along to Major General Deane, two days ago, and have not as yet received an answer thereto. So, till then, I will add no more, but that I am, Your servant, as occasion offers, – George Ogilvy

Shortly after this, Cromwell's Major General Deane forwarded to Ogilvy an unlikely letter from the Earl Marschall, praising his captors and authorising the surrender:

Loving friend, – since I received the favour of the liberty of the City of London from the Council of State … I find it my happiness to have to do with persons of so much honour, and justness that I am resolved to put my person, fortunes, houses and all freely in to their hands that I may peaceably enjoy myself and what belongs to me under the favour and protection of the Commonwealth of England. And in order hereunto, as conducing to my good, I do hereby require you to deliver up my house of Dunnottar to Major General Deane who is to receive the same from you in name of his Excellency My Lord General Cromwell for the use of the Commonwealth of England, whereof you must not fail. And, for so doing, this shall be your warrant, written and signed at my hand at London the 4th of May 1652, Your assured friend, – Marschall.

15 May 1652, Dunnottar – George Ogilvy to Major General Deane.

Sir, – I have received my Lord Marschall's letter about the rendition of this house, which I believe he could not refuse being a prisoner and possibly forced thereto by the Lord General, but seeing there are more concerned in this place than he, I cannot be satisfied therewith. Always to let you see how far I am for his good, and in no way contrary to yours, if it shall please you to procure liberty for my Lord Marschall to come to Scotland in freedom and not as prisoner, I shall be very much ruled by him, and upon honourable conditions, which I made known to you before by the Laird of Morphie, I shall be content to enter a capitulation, providing you remove your force from the Shire, and desist from further till his homecoming. If this seems not satisfactory, I must have patience and commit the event to the Lord to whose Providence I commit myself, and remain, Your servant, – George Ogilvie.

By this time, however, the heavy artillery had arrived and, after a siege which had lasted eight months, the Cromwellians were now able methodically to set about the reduction of Dunnottar. Seven lives were lost in a sustained bombardment but finally, on 24 May, an honourable capitulation was agreed by George Ogilvy:

24 May 1652, The camp, Blackhill – Articles of Agreement between Colonel Tho. Morgan on behalf of the Parliament of the Commonwealth of England, and Capt. George Ogilvy, Governor of Dunnottar Castle for the Surrender thereof.

1 – That the said Capt. Ogilvy deliver up to me the Castle of Dunnottar, with all the ordnance, arms, ammunition, provisions and all other utensils of war for the use of the Parliament of the Commonwealth of England, upon Wednesday the 26th instant by nine of the clock in the morning, without waste or embezzlement.

2 – That the late king's goods with the Lord Marschall's and all other goods within the said Castle shall be delivered to me or to whom I shall

appoint for the use of the Parliament of the Commonwealth of England.

3 – That the Crown and Sceptre of Scotland, together with all other Ensigns of Regality be delivered to me, or a good account thereof, for the use of the Parliament etc.

4 – That upon the true performance of the aforementioned articles, Capt. George Ogilvy, with the officers and soldiers under his command, shall have liberty to march forth of the said castle, at the hour appointed, with flying colours, drum beating, match lit, completely armed, the distance of one mile, there to lay down their arms, and to have passes to go to their own homes and there to live, without molestation, provided they act nothing prejudicial to the Commonwealth of England.

5 – That the said Capt. Ogilvy shall (free from sequestration) enjoy all the personal Estate which he has now without the Castle of Dunnottar, and all such necessary household stuff of his own which is now in the Castle, as shall be thought fit by me, or by them whom I shall authorize to deliver them unto him.

Tho. Morgan

As might be expected, Ogilvy's freedom was short lived; he and his wife were held prisoner in the castle for the rest of the year, interrogated at length, and subjected to threats of torture, all of which took its toll on the health of Elizabeth Douglas. (She died less than four years later, in April 1656).

28 December 1652 – General Dean to the [Cromwellian] Governor of Dunnottar Castle.
Warrant for Capt. Geo. Ogilvy's release from Dunnottar Castle upon bail.

Whereas, in the capitulation made upon the surrender of Dunnottar Castle between Colonel Thomas Morgan and Capt. George Ogilvy, the then Governor, it was, amongst other things, agreed that Capt. George Ogilvy should deliver up the Crown, Sword and Sceptre of the recent king of Scots which was in his custody, or give a good account thereof.

And forasmuch as I have caused Capt. Ogilvy, ever since that time, to be retained a prisoner in the Castle for not delivering the Crown, Sword and Sceptre aforesaid, nor giving a good account thereof, now in regard he makes diverse pretences that the said Crown, Sword and Sceptre were taken away out of Dunnottar Castle without his knowledge and, lastly, said his wife conveyed the same to a gentleman that carried them to foreign parts, I am willing that, provided he shall procure good security of 2000 or 1500 bond that he shall render himself a true prisoner to you, upon demand, as also that his wife shall do the like, he should have his liberty out of the Castle unto his own house, being seated within some four miles of the same, provided he go not at all from his said house above three miles, And I do hereby authorize you to receive such bond of him, for his and his wives forth coming and thereupon to give him the liberty above mentioned for which this shall be your warrant. – Richard Deane.

In this fiction, that the honours had been carried abroad, the person to whom Ogilvy had referred was John Keith, the younger brother of the Earl Marshall. It is understood that it was John Keith who had taken Ogilvy's letter, written on 1 February, to the King in France. By his own account, he had met with a series of unfortunate incidents that prevented the delivery of the letter until 11 April. His departure for the Continent at the beginning of February certainly made the governor's story fairly plausible but, in the fullness of time, George Ogilvy, and even some of his descendants, would live to regret his having used John Keith's name.

Although every fortress in Scotland was now in English hands, there were still pockets of resistance all over the country. Secret meetings were being held and plans were being discussed as they tried to organise and to enlist support. Eventually the talk produced some action but, as might be expected, it was to be undermined by a lack of unity. This time, it was not religion; it really came down to a personality conflict. Glencairn's Uprising, as it was called, had started in 1653 on a very small scale. William Cunningham, Earl of Glencairn had been elected leader of the Royalist resistance. He was joined near Loch Ard, just west of Aberfoyle, firstly by his host for the muster, Graham of Duchray, who was able to field forty men; the tutor of MacGregor brought eighty. A few days later, Lord Kenmure arrived with forty horses; the Laird of MacNaughton came with twelve horses and sixty men; Colonel Blackadder brought thirty. Glencairn had amassed about 300 men before the news reached Colonel Kidd, the Cromwellian governor of Stirling Castle. Kidd's attempt to nip this small-scale rebellion in the bud completely backfired. Glencairn's men cut them off before they reached Aberfoyle and literally chased them back to Stirling Castle. Hearing that the local Cromwellian forces had been defeated now gave heart to many who had been too cautious to take up arms.

Glencairn's leadership, it has to be said, was only ever intended to be temporary in lieu of General John Middleton, then still in France with the King. A concerned Johnston of Warriston was later to write that Middleton, he had heard, had been given 'an absolute commission not only in military and civil affairs but also in ecclesiastical, with express power to depose and put out ministers.' By the time Middleton arrived to take over, however, Glencairn had earned the respect of officers and men alike. At a muster of their forces, now about 5,000, Glencairn's announcement that he would be handing over command to Middleton was not well received. The murmurs of discontent, the support for Glencairn, threatened to undermine Middleton's authority. It is hard not to see what happened next as being anything other than planned. At a grand dinner to honour the new commander, Glencairn had made a toast:

> My Lord General, you see what a gallant army these worthy gentlemen
> here present and I have gathered together, at a time when it could hardly
> be expected that any number durst meet together. These men have come
> out to serve His Majesty, at the hazard of their lives and all that is dear to
> them. I hope, therefore, you will give them all the encouragement to do
> their duty that lies in your power.

Sir George Munro, Middleton's lieutenant-general stood up and said that the men he had seen that day were nothing but thieves and robbers and before long he would bring a very different calibre of men to the field. The insult was calculated to achieve the greatest offence.

Glengarry was first to his feet but Glencairn held him back, telling him that the affront was more his. Glencairn, as expected, accepted the challenge but early the next morning Munro discovered that he had underestimated Glencairn's swordsmanship; he was severely wounded. The outcome of the duel, however, had still favoured Middleton who was now able to have Glencairn arrested. This led to yet another duel over the rights and wrongs of the first. One of Munro's friends, a Captain Livingston, was despatched in the first thrust by a descendant of the noble Lindsay family who had found himself obliged to take Glencairn's part. Lindsay was arrested and his court-martial and execution left a large proportion of the Royalist army with little more than contempt for their new commander.

In February 1654, the Earl Marschall's brother, John Keith, returned to Scotland. Having been told that the Ogilvies had used his name to throw the Cromwellians off the scent he went to Middleton and asked him for a bogus receipt for the Honours. The receipt was back-dated: 'at Paris, June 1652.' In the event of his capture, this would back up the story and save him from the ordeal of an unpleasant interrogation. Eventually, inevitably, Middleton's forces surrendered and Keith was included in the capitulation. When questioned by Cromwell's Colonel Cobbet as to whether or not he was the John Keith who had carried the Regalia to France, he was able to produce the receipt. The search for the Honours had long since lost its intensity but this finally brought it to a conclusion. It also opened a much less attractive chapter in the story of their preservation.

4 January 1655 – King Charles II to the Countess Marschall.

I have so much to thank you for that, for your sake, I mention no particulars; but am confident I shall live to see you, when we shall be merry, and comfort one another with the memory of what we have done and suffered, I choose rather to let you have these two or three lines from me than to suffer you to imagine that I know not how much I owe you. And if this acknowledgement miscarries, it can do you no harm, and you will some other way know that I am very heartily, Your most affectionate friend, – Charles R.

Chapter Three

The Restoration was celebrated in Edinburgh with free claret and outdoor feasts. There were bonfires, fireworks on the castle, and musicians trying their best to entertain amid a cacophony of bells, cheering multitudes, trumpets and drums. It was also reported that, around this time, there was an exodus of Scots of every rank and title heading south and descending upon London to congratulate the King and also to make known their willingness to serve the Crown ... in a suitably improved capacity. For those who had demonstrated their loyalty, it was a time of golden opportunity (and devil take the hindmost). The *Domestic Annals of Scotland* recounts that: 'His Majesty not being able to satisfy all, there did arise great heart-burnings, animosity, and envy among them.' A disagreement arose between the earl of Southesk and the Master of Gray over the sheriffship of Forfarshire and, in the ensuing duel, Southesk killed the Master of Gray outside London. And now, out of the noble actions of Christian Fletcher and James Grainger, arose one of the most acrimonious and ignoble disputes of all.

On 15 May 1660, ten days before the King put a foot on English soil, the Countess Dowager of Marschall wrote the first of a series of letters to James Grainger.

15 May, Bolshan [home of the Countess, near Brechin in the county of Angus].

> ... since it has pleased the Lord to restore our King to his just right and crowns, a work as far above all human reach as it is above our deserving, I am resolved to remove the Honours which are in your custody.

And, believe me, whenever his Majesty shall send me his order for disposing of them, both you and Barrass [Ogilvy] shall not want that praise and commendation which your loyalty and his both deserves. I have given orders to George Straton (my servant) to receive them and to tell you truly, though I have been very plain with Barrass in my intentions, yet I have not let him know I would remove them so soon, which I do not conceal upon any account from him but only to have it done without his knowledge for such reasons as I conceive is for his good at present. And I doubt not as you consider all things you will approve of it ... Hoping, ere long, you shall receive your own thanks from the right owner, I shall only add that you have obliged me for ever to be your most affectionate and constant friend, Sic Subscribitur, Marie Erskine.

It was absolutely the wrong way to deal with the Rev. James. If she thought she could count on his complicity in keeping Ogilvy in the dark, and for some unfathomable reason, Countess or no Countess, she was going to have to think again. George Straton had the unenviable task of returning to Bolshan with nothing to show other than Grainger's reply.

18 May – Countess to Grainger

... I am satisfied with what you write in relation to not obeying my desire. However, I am now so deeply engaged in the business, as this bearer will show you, that I must crave your pardon to tell you I have sent him to bring them away, though even against your will (but you may be confident it shall not be against your weal), so again I pray excuse my incivility in this, and I beseech you to keep to your resolution to see me, that I may let you know that I am well satisfied with your carriage at this time. Marie Erskine

The Countess's engaging use of alliteration was not quite enough to win over Grainger. Once again, he sent the messenger on his way. It is worth observing that Marie Erskine was not a lady who was accustomed to having her wishes ignored. That he had incurred her displeasure the first time, and that a further rebuff almost certainly infuriated her is beyond doubt, but it was second nature to the Countess not to allow her feelings to dictate her actions in the short term. It would, nonetheless, be a mistake to think that she would forget. For the present, the minister's refusal to part with the Honours meant no more than that a letter she was writing would have to be worded slightly differently.

Five days later on 23 May, King Charles II left Holland and set sail for Dover. On the same day, the Countess despatched her son John to London, carrying with him a letter to the King in which, after the obligatory expressions of humility and loyalty, she writes that she has left nothing that was in her power to do for the safety of the Honours, in which it has pleased God to assist her:

> the way of securing them is too tedious for a letter except that the gentleman in command of the Castle of Dunnottar discharged his duty very honestly by putting them in the hands of a person who showed himself worthy of so great a trust.
>
> As for the detail, the bearer of this letter, my son, John Keith – who, by claiming to have taken the Honours abroad, prevented what danger a further search might have made – will give Your Majesty a full relation of all concerning the same. To which my son, Marschall (being a prisoner in the Tower of London) was altogether ignorant until his return to Scotland … and seeing that his house and family have been loyal to their King, I must humbly entreat Your Majesty to look upon them with the eye of favour, as your loyal subjects. And seeing that it is not necessary that the honours should lie any longer in obscurity, Your Majesty will resolve how to dispose of them and that I may have Your Majesty's warrant for obeying the same, which shall be performed by her, who shall ever continue, Your Majesty's faithful loyal subject and humblest servant, Marie Erskine.

Ogilvy, meanwhile, had been visiting the Graingers and discussing the situation. Christian Fletcher and her husband had risked their lives to safeguard the Regalia. The Ogilvies had endured the best part of a year in the hands of the Cromwellians and yet had kept the secret. No one was expecting any reward. They had done what needed to be done, and without any thought beyond that, but the Graingers were completely in agreement with Ogilvy: if the Countess hoped, somehow, to have a mark of the King's gratitude for their work, it was beyond the pail.

On Thursday, 19 July, the Countess writes:

> … I must expostulate with you for your refusing to deliver the Honours. I am especially dissatisfied that you would give me no assurance when you were here. And now I will deal freely with you: I am resolved to have them, and have sent men to search and range your house for them, who I suppose will not return without them. And I shall only say this, which I desire you to believe, I do this neither from any intention to wrong anybody nor for advantage to myself but that, seeing his Majesty knows all about their preservation and believes that after my son John claimed to having taken them, and got Middleton's receipt, that they were in my custody, makes me take this course, which is all I shall say at this time, but I shall still be your very loving friend, Marie Erskine.

This met with no more success. Grainger still refused and the Countess's men had to return empty handed. The event, however, alarmed Ogilvy who felt sure that the men would soon be returning in greater numbers. He favoured removing the Honours to his own property.

Saturday, 21 July, Kinneff – James Grainger to Ogilvy.

> For his honoured and loving friend, The Laird of Barrass, elder.
> Sir, I have received yours and, before it came to my hand, I had secured the things you know of upon the night time and I am persuaded, though an army should come, they could not be safer, so there is nothing to fear. As for my self, my neck shall break and my life go before I fail to you, yet some little difficulty makes me loath they should be transported as yet and this shall be fully made known to you at our meeting which I

desire shall be on Monday. If you are loath to come here, send me word
and I shall come to you. But for the business itself, fear no more than if
they were in your own house, for I trust he who has preserved them in
my custody till this day will preserve them in safety till they go as you
yourself desire. So till our meeting I continue, Your real and true friend,

Mr James Grainger

Monday's meeting did not go too well for George Ogilvy. He had
decided that the safest course was to place himself in possession of the
Honours, but he now found that the minister could not be persuaded
to part with them, even to him. Had Ogilvy still been the governor
of Dunnottar and acting under the Earl Marschall's commission, there
would have been nothing to prevent Grainger from handing them back.
That not being the case, however, Grainger felt he should play it by the
book. His main defence for having refused the Countess was to be able
to say that he would surrender the Regalia to no one other than the Earl
Marschall himself. It would, in fact, have served Ogilvy just as well but
unfortunately after the meeting, presumably in the company of someone he knew well, he let his exasperation get the better of him and said
what he really thought of the minister's sense of propriety. Whatever he
said, it found its way to the Countess in a matter of hours and it gave her
exactly what she needed. She could see that this heavy-handed approach
was getting her nowhere. She knew that she needed to change tack and
now, courtesy of Ogilvy, she had been handed an opportunity to divide
and conquer. Before the day was out, she had written to Grainger:

Monday, 23 July.

I am more sorry for the trouble you have had than that I miss of my
desire, but I could not have expected such expressions from Barrass as
I hear he had both of you and me. When he thinks better on what he
said − and I have written in the enclosed − he will find (I hope) he has
mistaken my intentions. I have been too instrumental of his good to seek
his ruin; but it seems he has forgotten bygones, which I cannot do. I hope

you will excuse my troubling you so often, and I promise you I shall not hereafter desire them out of your custody till the Kings pleasure be known, which would ever content me. And I hope he knows everyone's part, and I may say I never lessened either Barrass's or your parts but, in the first place, expressed them, as he knows himself. I shall trouble you no more, but am your very loving and assured friend, – Marie Erskine

This hit the mark. Whatever Grainger read in 'the enclosed' he was adequately offended. He now saw George Ogilvy in a different light and he began to wonder if he had misjudged the Countess.

On 1 August, she writes to the minister:

I received your last, wherein you give me a very particular relation of Barrass's desires to you that day after Gibbie left you, and I shall say nothing as to how needless were his apprehensions that I was to send a stronger party, but shall leave you to consider it; for truly I never conceived any prejudice to me by your keeping of them till his Majesty's pleasure be known, nor yet was my desire to have them from any advantage I could have in having them here beside me but, as I showed you before, I believe the King thought that they were in my custody and, in being so, I think it was but reason, all being considered. And as for Barrass having let some tears fall, truly I understand it not what could occasion them. I take God to witness I had no thoughts of any prejudice to him … As for your part, I am satisfied because you did ingenuously show me how you were surprised and even ensnared, first in removing the Honours, which he never told me, though desired by you, and last, in making you give an oath to him, who had no power to take it, and all the time keeping an underhand way with me; but I leave this. If it be in my power to do anything that may express my sense of your honest and free way with me, you shall find it. And seeing Barrass had again appointed to be at your house on Friday last, I desire by this bearer to know what his desires were, and what past between you and him. I wish you had some good errand to bring you again to my house in Angus, that I might show you how really I am your truly loving friend, Marie Erskine.

These past few weeks, George Ogilvy had been receiving advice from friends and relations: instead of complaining to them about the Countess, he should be following her example; she is looking after her family's interests – he should be doing the same. They urged him not to waste any more time and to get himself off to London to present his own case to the King. Ogilvy, however, was reluctant to leave Scotland for fear of what might happen to the Regalia in his absence. Eventually, he sent his son William to stay in London and await the first opportunity to have his petition presented at Court.

On 4 September, the King wrote to the Countess:

Madam, I am so sensible of the good service done to me in preserving my Crown, Sceptre and Sword, that as I have put marks upon your sons, so I could not let them go to Scotland without acknowledging also my sense of your kindness and care in that and other things relating to my service during my absence. I do desire that the Honours may be delivered to my Lord Marschall that, as he received them, so they may be delivered by him to the ensuing Parliament, and shall only add that on all occasions you shall find me, your affectionate friend, Charles R.

The marks to which the King referred were, firstly, that the Earl Marschall was now to become Lord Privy Seal and, regarding his young brother, John, the Writer to the Great Seal of Scotland was ordered to record that:

… His Majesty having perfect knowledge of the worth and loyalty of John Keith, brother to the Earl Marschall, whereof he has given good testimony at every occasion during the late troubles, and of the great service he performed in the entire preserving of his Majesty's Royal Honours, the Crown, Sword and Sceptre, from the violence and possession of these rebels that these years past had overrun and possessed themselves of his Majesty's kingdom of Scotland, a service never to be forgotten by succeeding generations, and which doth so justly entitle him to some honourable employment in his Majesty's service. His Majesty hath therefore of his certain knowledge made, constituted and created, and, by these presents, makes constitutes and creates the said John Keith Knight Marschall of the Kingdom of Scotland and gives and grants to him, all the days of his lifetime, the place and office of Knight Marschall of Scotland, with power to him to exercise and discharge the same and to enjoy all the privileges, benefits, dignities and others due and belonging thereunto … And in regard of his constant attendance at Parliaments and other occasions of his Majesty's service, his Majesty has given and granted and annexed and, by the tenor hereof, gives grants and annexes unto the said office, a yearly pension of £400 sterling for all the years of his lifetime, to be paid out of the readiest of his Majesty's rents, customs or casualities of his Exchequer … commanding hereby his Majesty's Treasurers … and all others whom it concerns, to make exact and punctual payment of this pension accordingly …

It was to be a very long time before the news of John Keith's knighthood reached Kinneff. A calm had descended upon the manse, the Countess having apparently retracted her desire to get the Regalia away from the minister. Ogilvy had been wrong about her; the 'stronger party' were never sent to search the Graingers' property. Things were getting back to normal and, for several weeks, they had been left in peace. And then, incredibly, an Act of Parliament appeared.

19 September 1660

The Committee of Estates being informed that the Crown, Sceptre and Sword, which are the ancient Honours of this, His Majesty's kingdom, have, in their times of trouble bygone, been safely preserved by Mr James Grainger, minister at Kinneff, and Christian Fletcher, his wife: And that the said Mr James is desirous that the same should now be taken off his hands, and delivered to such persons of trust as the Committee shall appoint for that effect. They do hereby give order and warrant to Sir Gilbert Ramsay of Balmayne, elder, and James Peadie, baillie of Montrose, to repair to the said Mr James and, in the name of the Committee, render him thanks for his careful preservation of the said Honours and show him that they will, with best conveniency, effectually recommend him to the Parliament, that a gratuity for his pains may be given him; and to receive from him the foresaid Honours, and make particular inventory thereof; whereabout and for delivery of the said Honours, these presents [this writing] shall be to the said Mr James a sufficient warrant and exoneration.

This Act was accompanied by an order for Robert Keith, the Earl Marschall's uncle who, after Alyth, had taken the key of the strongroom to the Countess:

The Committee of Estates do hereby give, order and warrant to Robert Keith of Whiteriggs, Sheriff Depute to the Earl Marschall, to receive from Sir Gilbert Ramsey of Balmayne and James Peadie, baillie of Montrose, the Honours of this kingdom, viz. Crown, Sceptre and Sword, and to preserve them in his custody within the Castle of Dunnottar, until the Earl Marschall return from England, or till further order from the said Committee or Estates of Parliament, whereabout these presents shall be his warrant.

The said Mr James, as it happened, was not in the least desirous that the Honours should be taken off his hands. The minister, to the astonishment of all concerned, more or less told them to go forth and multiply. Marie Erskine had almost exhausted every possible avenue. Even an Act of Parliament had now failed to achieve James Grainger's compliance. She could not have him arrested without the whole county, and ultimately the King, becoming aware of the fabrication on which her ambitions had been founded. It seemed that the immovable object had triumphed over the irresistible force but, when it came to lateral thinking, the Countess proved once again to be in a class of her own. She could not get her hands on the Regalia but it dawned on her that she could claim that Grainger was acting under her instructions and that he was holding on to the Honours, on her behalf. On the 28th, a further Act, rescinding the previous Act, states that the Committee of Estates is now:

> ... more fully informed that the Honours are in the custody of Mr James Grainger, as trusted and employed in the preservation thereof by the Countess of Marshall who, having received from the said Earl, her son, the key of that closet in the Castle of Dunnottar in which the said Honours lay, in order to ensure their preservation, contrived and ordered the safe conveyance of the said Honours out of the said castle (before it was rendered) and the committing thereof to the trust and custody of the said Mr James, as a person in whom she reposed during the absence and imprisonment of her said son. And now that the said Earl has an order and warrant from his Majesty to the Countess, his mother, to deliver back to him the said Honours, to be preserved in the said Castle, till his Majesty or Parliament further order thereabout: And thereupon, the said Committee finding no necessity of their two orders abovementioned; therefore the said Committee do hereby recall and rescind their said two former orders, and leave the said Honours to be called for and disposed of by the said Earl, according to the trust and orders of Parliament, whereby the same were committed to him and his Majesty's warrant abovementioned.

While the Committee of Estates were busy enshrining the Countess's story in Scots Law, George Ogilvy was visiting the Kinneff manse and explaining to Grainger the absolute dire necessity of his having possession of at least some part of the Regalia. Somehow, he managed to persuade the minister to part with the Sceptre.

On this same day, Ogilvy's petition, proclaiming him as the sole preserver of the Honours, was finally presented at court by the efforts of Lord Airlie. Charles II found this a bit confusing. Not only had he heard this story before, albeit with a different cast, but on the strength of what he had been told the first time around he had already created John Keith Knight Marschall of Scotland. The King said: 'by my Lord's good leave, it must not be so, for my Lady Marshall wrote to me that she and her son, John, had preserved the Honours.' The Earl of Lauderdale was on hand to step into the breach. There was, he offered, a simple solution. On Lauderdale's suggestion, the King issued an order for George Ogilvy to deliver the Regalia to the Earl Marshall and to get a receipt from him. Ogilvy was in danger of losing everything. If he can produce the receipt, he will get some credit for his part in the business but, if not – and it would be assumed by all those in the know that he could not – both his name and his prospects will be ruined. Such were the stakes that hung on this piece of paper. It did not seem to interest anyone that the true preservers of the Scottish Crown Jewels, the minister and his wife, had never even been in the running.

By October, the Earl Marschall was back in Scotland.

2 October 1660, Countess Marschall to Grainger.

I shall not need, with this, to give any particular answer to your last, only I must say you and Barrass are not well met. But I hope, now, all parties will be satisfied that my son Marschall has brought me a letter from his Majesty that the Crown, etc. may be delivered to him. And, for your further satisfaction, I have given the King's letter to the bearer, Whiteriggs, to be shown to you, being confident that you will deliver the Crown, Sceptre and Sword to any that my son shall desire you to give them unto, which will free you of further trouble seeing they are to lie in Dunnottar till they be called for. And besides that it will be an exoneration to you, it will oblige my son and me both to deal for all the favour we can to be put upon you for your faithful service in this trust. Marie Erskine

During this visit to Bolshan, his mother's house, the Earl Marschall would hear pretty much the same tale that he had already been told by his brother John, by Middleton, and by the Countess's other friends in London. He would also hear some account of the tedious minister's anxiety over parting with the honours without competent authority; the man's veneration for protocol was bordering on the impertinent. The following day, he wrote to Grainger.

3 October 1660, Bolshan, William, Earl of Marschal, to James Grainger.

Knowing that the Crown and Honours of this kingdom are yet continued in your custody, and that it is now altogether necessary that they be
taken off your hands and secured in my house of Dunnottar conform
to his Majesty's will, which he has sent by an express to my Lady, my
mother, for delivering of them to me; and there being a prior warrant
from my Lord Chancellor and Council of Estate direct to Sir Gilbert
Ramsey of Balmaine and James Peadie in Montrose to receive the honours from you which, upon better information, is recalled, and a new
order directed to you for delivering the same to me or any I shall entrust,
I do therefore hereby desire you to deliver the said Crown, Sceptre and
Sword according to the inventory lying beside them, to Robert Keith of
Whiteriggs, who has the charge of my house of Dunnottar, that they may
be transported there by him before my coming that length. And I assure
you I shall be very willing in concurring that special notice shall be taken
of your good service in the care and preservation of them. This being all
till meeting, I rest your very affectionate friend, Marschall.

Whiteriggs had been at the minister's door before so, if he was to turn
up again, he would know what to expect. On Saturday, 6 October, however, the Earl Marschall visited his daughter at Arbuthnott. An altogether
different set of family connections now came into play. After Elizabeth
Douglas's death in 1655, George Ogilvy had married Margaret Arbuthnott,
daughter of Arbuthnott of Fiddes and, in 1658, the Earl Marschall's daughter, Elizabeth, had married Robert, 2nd Viscount Arbuthnott. Now, for the
first time, the Earl Marschall was to hear something much closer to the
truth or at least closer to George Ogilvy's version of events. He also came
to understand something of Ogilvy's current predicament. He agreed that
Ogilvy should have his receipt. They realised, however, that it could not be
given in Grainger's presence; the minister, still completely unaware of the
situation and ramifications, would naturally expect the receipt to come to
him. It was decided, therefore, to post-date Ogilvy's receipt for Monday
but to give it to him before the actual handover of the Honours:

At Dunnottar, the 8th day of October 1660, I, William, Earl Marschall, grant me to have received, from George Ogilvy of Barrass, the Crown, Sword and Sceptre, the ancient monuments of this kingdom, entire and complete and in the same condition they were entrusted by me to him, and discharge the aforesaid George Ogilvy of his receipt thereof by this my subscription, day and place foresaid, – Marschall.

On Saturday, 6 October, a very-much-relieved George Ogilvy writes to Grainger:

Please find the enclosed from my Lord Marschall. It is his desire that you and I should meet him at Dunnottar on Monday by 12 o' clock. Therefore be pleased to meet me at Barrass by 10 o' clock and bring these things you have with you and I shall do the like, and we shall both go together and wait upon his Lordship and deliver them of our hands to himself who has promised very fair. But I have many things to speak to you at meeting. I pray you be careful they fall not by the way. This is all for the present but that I am and ever shall be your real friend and bound servant, George Ogilvy.

Let these present my love to your wife and all yours.

(Enclosed) Saturday, 6 October – Earl Marschall to Grainger

Right Reverend, these are desiring you that you would meet me at Dunnottar upon Monday the eighth of this instant by twelve o'clock that I may receive the Honours there, where they were left formerly by me, where Barrass has promised to meet, where I may give you both your due thanks, and at meeting I shall more fully express myself. So till then and ever I rest, Marschall.

On the Monday, with Ogilvy present, and in the company of several witnesses, Grainger handed over the Regalia at Dunnottar. He requested a receipt from the Earl Marshall and he was told, in effect, he would get it later. Shortly after this, the Earl Marschall wrote to his mother, the Countess:

Madam, I can not write to your Ladyship all the passages I have found in receiving the Honours in this little time I have been from you. For since the business is at a point, and they now in my custody, I leave to say further therein except that it has been an ugly and unhandsome-carried business ... I desire your Ladyship would send me that letter of William Ogilvy or the double thereof. My wife would have written to your Ladyship but she has nothing more to say than I have written. She is your Ladyship's humble servant and I am still Madam, Your Ladyship's most obedient son and humble servant, – Marschall

At this point, incredible as it may seem with hindsight, Grainger still has no idea that the Keiths and the Ogilvies are competing for advancement in rank and title. James Grainger's friendship with Ogilvy had been based on trust, a trust that had been badly dented when the Countess had been able to report what Ogilvy had said about him. Living that bit nearer to Kinneff and being able, therefore, to meet Grainger more often, Ogilvy had managed to regain some ground but, even so, Grainger felt he could never completely trust him again. It had shaken his faith in human nature. He was a man who preferred to see things in black and white and he was really ill-equipped to deal with the shades of slightly grubby grey that had been intruding upon his world. Ogilvy, however, was about to make things easier for him.

14 October 1660, Bolshan – Marie Erskine, Countess Dowager of Marschal, to Grainger.

I received your letter and thank you for it, and I am only sorry that you and I both have so much trusted that man, who gives us now still more experience of his craftiness and falsehood. For what you tell me he has been saying to you are, for the most part, flat lies. Indeed for his son's petitioning for him at London, we were informed of that before, by a letter from his son to him, which my son, I believe, has acquainted him with, since the honours were received. And that, I know, is the thing that most moves him to rage: when he sees his main draught discovered. But as for his alleging he has got a receipt from my son, I am confident it is a lie. But I hope you will now be more wise than to be further tempted by him to your own hurt. I have written to my son of his untrue aversions to you, and also of your care to acquaint me with them; which I hope he will consider. But wishing to see you shortly, according to your promise, I shall forbear other particulars, only I am very sensible of your kindness, which I trust you shall have no cause to repent you of.

(P.S.) He but abuses you when he says he has obtained my son's favour. I assure you there is no such thing. Marie Erskine

It had been obvious to the Rev. Grainger that, for some time, either Ogilvy or the Countess was not being straight with him. That they could both be using him was too far beyond the bounds of credibility. But, at last, it all seemed to be falling into place. Now he understood why the Countess had wished to remove the Honours so soon and why, 'for his own good', she had not told Ogilvy: she had suspected Ogilvy from the start although, being a lady of discretion, she had not voiced her suspicions. The man's self-serving ambition now being fully exposed, Grainger was appalled that Ogilvy should have so completely surrendered to his base instincts, making a pretence of friendship in order to pursue his own selfish agenda. From this point forward, a very angry (and naïve) James Grainger launched himself, wholeheartedly, into a sustained attack on George Ogilvy. The following declaration, the last paragraph of which could almost have been written by Marie Erskine herself, was sent to her by Grainger on 19 October. She subsequently forwarded it to Middleton in London.

Being informed that George Ogilvy of Barrass has his son at London, giving out that his father was the only preserver of the Honours of Scotland, when they were in hazard to be taken, and that they were in his custody ever since, although others have been more instrumental than he; I thought good therefore to declare the truth, viz. that in August 1651, by the Countess of Marschal the Honours were delivered to George Ogilvy with charge to him to secure them, and he keeping them in Dunnottar till there was no probability of longer maintaining the castle, he employed me, having sufficient assurance of my loyalty to His Majesty, and fidelity in promise-keeping, to carry the Honours out of the house, and secure them. And to bar suspicion, I sent my wife who brought them forth without being discovered by the enemy, although rancountred by them in the way. This was in the beginning of March 1652; And he, having engaged me that, with all conveniency, I should go and acquaint my Lady Marschall therewith, in the end of March, I went and informed her of the whole procedure, which she approved of and was satisfied that they should remain in my keeping, taking also my ticket of having them, expressing the particular place where they were secured.

So that I have kept them according to her desire till this present October 1660, the eight day of which at my Lady's command, and according to the order she had received from his Majesty, for that effect in Dunnottar Castle, I delivered them to the Earl Marschal, before these witnesses: the Viscount of Arbuthnott, the Sheriff-depute of the Mearns and several other gentlemen, whereupon I required a ticket of receipt but was deferred till afterward, since which time, I am informed that George Ogilvy has obtained, from the Earl Marschall, a receipt, and sent either it or the double of it to London to be produced by his son, as if the Honours had been in his custody, and by him preserved, although it be well known to his son that I had them in my house and keeping ever since the first delivery of them to me.

But indeed the prime means of their safety was the declaring them to be carried off the kingdom by the Earl Marschall's brother John for as it stopped the enemy from searching for them, so it freed George Ogilvy from prison and further trial. In witness of the truth, I have written and subscribed these presents with my hand, the nineteenth of October 1660 years, Sic Subscribitur, James Grainger.

12 *November 1660, Kinneff – James Grainger to the Countess.*

Madam, I could not of duty omit to write to your Ladyship at this time, for Barrass is now offering at high things, namely to improve against your Ladyship. He has written to his Majesty about the Honours, I do not write by information, but he told me it out of his own mouth. I shall not now insist on particulars but, for preventing any inconveniency, I will write in general, for he thought to have drawn me on to concur in the plot, for he feared without me he would not get any things gone about rightly. But I have given up all dealings with him in that way. His son is in London and has written to him that my Lord Ogilvy [Airly] has gone with him to his Majesty, and has declared that his father did preserve the Honours and offered, notwithstanding all your Ladyship had written to his Majesty, that they were yet in his father's hands, and has good hopes as he has written to his father of great things.

He writes that if the Honours are not yet delivered that neither any Lord nor Lady in the Kingdom, should get them till he writes again; even if they have an order from his Majesty. But since that was not now to be helped, he told me what course he should take, namely that he would show a ticket of receipt subscribed by the Earl Marschal that he had received the Honours from him. I enquired where he got that and when he had got it, seeing I delivered them, and he refused to give me a ticket of receipt. 'Oh,' said he, 'I got it the night before by means of my Lord Arbuthnott.' Truly, I thought it very strange. Now I did refuse to concur with him till I heard all. And then I told him I would not be deceived any more with him. And your Ladyship remembers I did ever fear he would easily wind himself in my Lord Marschall's favour. Your Ladyship may make the best use hereof your Ladyship can. Barrass is very busy to post away his letters to his son, for he told me he was presently going to Newgrange to dispatch his letters in haste. I continue, Madam, Your Ladyship's humble servant, Sic Subscribitur, Mr J Grainger

P.S. Madam, It is easy to improve him, both that it was I that delivered the Honours and at your Ladyships direction, and likewise that his discharge was written the day before they were delivered, I hope to see your Ladyship next week God-willing.

It is to be assumed that her Ladyship did indeed make the best use of Grainger's information about the post-dated receipt. She would consider it far from ideal to have Ogilvy in a position to move in society, broadcasting his version of the story to all who would listen.

15 November 1660, London – Earl of Middleton to the Countess Marschall.

Madam, I most humbly, in the first place, crave your Ladyship's pardon, for not returning particular answers to your letters. Your son, my noble friend, when he was in this place, did save me the labour and really, Madam, I cannot one day be master of an hour of time. I am both sorry and ashamed that so little a person as Mr Ogilvy should have put your Ladyship to so much trouble, and I am struck with amazement to think that my Lord Marschall should in the least countenance him. I shall not be wanting to put a stop to his pretensions, and serve you with as much faithfulness and zeal as any servant you have. And, really, it has ever been my ambition to be accounted among the number of your servants, and I hope all my actions shall express that I am, Madam, Your Ladyship's most faithful obedient humble servant, – Middleton.

In the end, in spite of all efforts to undermine his claim, George Ogilvy was not denied his reward. His receipt proved that he had, after all, been involved in some way. He was given a baronetcy and his lands of Barrass were converted from ward holding to blanch for an annual payment of one penny. Ogilvy's pension was for £200 sterling per year.

In spite of her feelings towards Grainger on account of his repeated obdurate refusal to comply with her wishes, the Countess graciously offered to help the Graingers apply to Parliament for a token of his Majesty's gratitude. Unfortunately, it seems something went astray in the process of the Act being committed to paper and, consequently, James Grainger's name failed to appear in the Act; it credited only his wife, Christian Fletcher.

January 1661 – Act of the Parliament of Scotland in favour of Mrs Grainger.

At Edinburgh the eleventh day of January jm vjc and sextie one years. Forasmuch as the Estates of Parliament do understand that Christian Fletcher, spouse to Maister James Grainger, minister at Kinneff, was most active in conveying the royal honours, his Majesty's Crown, Sword, and Sceptre, out of the castle of Dunnottar immediately before it was rendered to the English usurpers, and that by her care the same were hid and preserved; therefore the King's Majesty, with advice of his Estates of Parliament; do appoint two thousand marks Scotts [a one-off payment of £111 sterling] to be forthwith paid unto her by his Majesty's Treasurer out of the readiest of his Majesty's rents, as a testimony of their sense of her service aforementioned.

No one could be blamed for seeing the Countess's hand behind this omission and yet, if she did see to it that Grainger's part was left out, it may have had nothing to do with spite. In his own submission, the minister would necessarily have explained that, at Ogilvy's request, he had contrived and arranged the method of the removal of the Honours from Dunnottar. But that statement could hardly be allowed to stand since it was now written into an Act of the Scottish Parliament that it had been the Countess who had 'contrived and ordered the safe conveyance of the said Honours out of the said castle ... and the committing thereof to the trust and custody of the said Mr James, as a person in whom she reposed during the absence and imprisonment of her said son.' Christian Fletcher went to Bolshan to confront the Countess, asking her why, given that her husband's submission had been absolutely clear on the chain of events, his name had been omitted from the Act. Chrissie did not quite share her husband's reverence for her Ladyship and reading between the lines of a subsequent letter, it looks as if the Countess could see a time coming when she might need to practice her 'divide and conquer' technique on the Graingers.

5 April 1661, Bolshan – Countess to James Grainger.

I received yours by this bearer, and if it had not been for my Lord's sickness which has been dangerous till within this eight days, you would have heard from me when I came home. But now, the Provincial drawing near, I hoped you should, from thence, visit friends, so I resolved not to write till I saw if you came. But for answer to your letter, in the first, you thank me for my kindness in writing on your behalf. Truly I was obliged to do it and more if it had been in my power. Before my coming there, your wife had done your business, and indeed when she came and showed me that act, I was no ways satisfied, for neither was the reward answerable to your deserving nor was that act rightly set down. That I admired of and spoke my thoughts freely to some, as you shall know at meeting.

I hope your wife will not say that she found me offended at anything except that you were so slighted, nor did I find any speeches of your wife to give me offence. I wonder upon what ground you could write any such thing to me. You remember I ever wished you had gone yourself, nor was there such haste necessary; but all being done and the Act passed before I came, I could go no further. But I leave all till we meet.

I knew nothing of Barrass's return till I read your letter. Before I came home it was reported he was knight baronet, which is no great business. For the holding of his lands blanch, I suppose he holds them of the Marquess of Douglas, that hardly the King can do it. For his pension of £200 sterling, if there no greater errand but that that gentleman discovers your name in your letter, it may be the pension prove not so great, and, if any, I am sure it has been procured upon his large expenses, say what he will. As for my warning him from Craigie, [Ogilvy owned Barrass, but lived in Craigie] I know he has my liferent of it, but I have only given the warning that I may see his assedatione for reasons you shall know, for the double I had of it was lost when Fetteresso was burnt. I know the man's temper, he will … at pleasure, but a little time will make him better composed. I had this unworthy token for you at my being in … which I hope you will take in good part as a small remembrance of a great kindness for you as long as I live; and let me entreat you neither to believe nor be moved for any speeches of Barrass's. In a short time he will perhaps forget his ranting discourse, I assure you too many of them boasts. I showed how he circumvened and abused both you and me, and I believe no honest people will think the better of, for all his knighthood. Sometime when I send north you shall hear from me, who shall ever be your very loving friend, (sic subscribitur) Marie Erskine.

Throughout most of 1661, the Countess and the minister remained on good terms, united in their condemnation of Ogilvy and their desire to bring him to justice.

26 August 1661, Bolshan – Countess to James Grainger.

I expected to have heard from you before now that I might have sent you some sugar; and, having occasion to send this bearer north, I have sent you a box with some. As winter pass you shall have more. And I wish I had anything would do you good, for, believe me, it should be very heartily given. The bearer will tell you how high the new knight hath carried. He may live to repent his carriage to me. He is very busy in giving information for to verify himself, as the bearer will tell you, of his being with the Lord Hackertown. It's a wonder how he hath the impudence to say that my Lord Marschall did entrust the honours to him and so how could he but deliver them to him. What you hear you will let me know. So for this time and ever I am your very loving and assured friend, (sic subscribitur) Marie Erskine.

11 October 1661, Bolshan – Countess to James Grainger.

According to your desire I have sent you not only those two letters you desire, but also Whiteriggs letter to Barrass and Barrass to you before these were written by my son to you the day before you delivered the Honours; as also I have sent you a true copy of your declaration which went to England, because you told me you could not lay your hands on that which you kept. That gentleman soars very high, as I hear, but maybe he will land low. I am exceedingly glad of your recovery. I hope you and I shall live to see those who have miscarried to us sensible of their fault. I have directed the bearer as he comes here any time to come by you for I shall be glad to hear from you; and so being in haste I must end, but am ever your very loving and assured friend, Marie Erskine.

16 October 1661, Bolshan – Countess to James Grainger.

I received yours with this bearer, and how soon you have leisure to draw up that paper you may be pleased to send it, that I may see it. I believe neither you nor I aim at anything but to clear truth, and discover that man's untruths. I admire his impudence in saying I had given you that money. I cannot believe that George Straton would assert any such thing as that he delivered or numbered 500 merks which you received, it being so gross an untruth. However, I shall put him to it, and shall have the truth under his hand, which ere long you shall see. As for Barrass going to dwell in Edinburgh, I hope he will live there like a baronet, but for his complaint to his master (whom he calls the old good man) I fear it not, nor am I seeking anything from him that is his, and what is my own I intend to crave. My Lords condition keeps me from the Mearns. If I were sometimes there, I hope he would at least speak less. I wish you good health and some good occasion that I might see you. So, with my good wishes to your wife, I remain, &c., Marie Erskine

Around this time, the resourceful Countess had got her hands on a copy of Ogilvy's petition. She sent it to Grainger who, glad of the chance to renew his crusade against the evil Ogilvy, dutifully delineated every apparent lie and half-truth, answering them, line by line (q.v. Supplementary Papers no.8). The Countess reviewed Grainger's comments, made some edits and sent him the updated version (q.v. Supplementary Papers no.8).

28 October 1661, Bolshan – Countess to James Grainger.

Having occasion to send this bearer north, I resolved to make him the carrier of these and, as I promised, I here send you my thoughts of the paper you sent me, whose substance is the same with yours, only I conceive this [q.v. Supplementary Papers no.9] to be the best way in answering his untruths particularly; but you may mend what you find amiss or not well-worded, and when you think it right, you will write it over your self and set your name to it, and send a double to me, with these letters of mine and Barrass, which I last sent to you. Who knows, but it may please God yet that we make that deceitful man's doings known even to his Majesty, but it must be well-timed, and kept very secret, which I doubt not you will do. I will be glad to know what the gentleman that said to you he heard George Straton tell these untruths, say when he sees George's letter to me. I would be very glad if your informer would stand to it. Till I hear from you I will say no more, but I shall ever continue, &c., Marie Erskine

As far as can be determined, the correspondence ceased completely at this point. It is impossible to explain this without resorting to conjecture but, on the other hand, arguably, the only mystery is that it lasted this long. The minister's outrage at Ogilvy's deception would be utterly eclipsed by his reaction to the news that the Countess had been successful in getting her son, John Keith, the title of Knight Marschall of Scotland but there is, as yet, no letter or documentation to be found establishing the moment in time when that news was broken to Grainger. What is known is this: James Grainger died in the week preceding 20 May 1663, having received neither recognition nor reward. Some time after his death, however, Christian Fletcher submitted the following declaration to Parliament:

The Royal honours of this kingdom, after his Majesty's Coronation at Scone, were secured by the Earl of Marschall in his Castle of Dunnottar and thereafter his lordship, being taken prisoner by the English at Alyth, was brought to go aboard a ship but obtained liberty for his natural uncle Robert Keith of Whiteriggs to go to the Mearns about his affairs, and so privately did give him the key of his closet wherein the Honours were and desired him to give the key to my lady dowager, his mother, then dwelling in Bolshan to the effect she might go along with him to take out the Honours for securing of them from the English who were, at that time, in that Shire, which she did, but finding difficulty and hazard to take them out, in respect the English were lying in Stanehive within less than half a mile to Dunnottar, she delivered the Honours to George Ogilvy of Barrass, then Governor of that Castle to be kept by him till she should find out a way to bring them from thence, which could not be done, in respect the number of the English daily increased, going thence for Inverness and coming south.

My deceased husband having to do with the Governor George Ogilvy (he being one of the heritors of his parish) went to Dunnottar where the said Governor did show to him the Royal Honours and, having seen them, he desired the Governor to have a particular care of them, the preservation of them being of great consequence. The impression of the words did so take the Governor that, he having revealed the discourse to his deceased wife Elizabeth Douglas, they did conclude that they would send for me and entrust me with the keeping of them. And immediately thereafter I had a letter from the said Elizabeth Douglas whereupon I went to Dunnottar five miles distant from my house and after a little conference with the said Elizabeth Douglas, she showed me the honours desiring me to take upon me the keeping of them and to carry them along with me, which I by the Lord's assistance did willingly undertake. Whereupon she delivered to me the Crown and Sceptre which I brought with me on horseback riding always near to the sea, along the tops of high craggs, resolving rather to lose my life and throw them in the sea than that they should have taken them from me, being at the time in fears of the enemy always. By the Lord's providence I brought them to my house and that night, when my family were asleep, my husband and I went to the kirk and, having wrapped them in cloths, we interred them.

This was done by me in the month of February after the fight at Worcester and thereafter in the month of March, I went with my servant on foot and brought away the sword in a sackfull of hards [coarse flax tow] upon my servant's back, and came through the English with the hazard of my life and brought it also to my house and interred it, no person knowing where they were interred but my deceased husband and I, and immediately thereafter I went and brought away the case of the sword in a sackfull of cods [pillows], having folded it in two because of its length and greatness.

And so, having brought all away and buried them in the kirk, my husband and I went every three months and did take them up and aired them in the night-time before a fire. And having wrapped them in new cloth, interred them again. This we did continually till his Majesty's happy and gracious restoration. My deceased husband, by reason of his long indisposition, being for many years on the dying hand, resolved to reveal it to the Countess Dowager of Marschall where the Honours were lying and, having taken her oath of secrecy, he gave it under his hand where they were lying.

Dunnottar being taken in by the English, they demanded the Governor and his lady what had become of the Honours. His lady replied that she had delivered them to John Keith, son to the said Dowager and that she had his receipt which she showed to Major General Morgan. And, thereafter, John Keith having come back to Scotland from Holland, his mother, apprehending he might be in hazard, sent him to the Earl of Middleton who was in the hills, and so procured from him a receipt as if they had been delivered in Holland, and produced it to Colonel Cobbet.

And no more hand Sir John Keith had in preserving the Honours than is here said nor no person else but my husband and I till they were delivered to the Earl of Marschall in Dunnottar, the eighth of October 1660, in accordance with his letter, in as good condition as we received them, with the inventory lying beside them.

This declaration, containing the first reference to 'Sir' John Keith from either of the Graingers, hardly hints at the sense of injustice and betrayal that preceded it. There is no way to date it except that it was written after James Grainger's death although, possibly, by looking at Christian Fletcher's circumstances, we can hazard a guess. At the end of May 1663, she had lost her husband and her home. By the following month, she has to consider that she has no income; she has one eighteen-year-old son, John, at university; Robert, fourteen, is at school; she has her youngest, seven-year-old James, to take care of; and she now discovers that she is pregnant. Set this against Sir John Keith's pension of £400 per year for the rest of his life and Sir George Ogilvy's annual pension of £200, and her motivation for penning the declaration is a matter of reasonable inference.

Once again, however, this story, which had been shrouded in mystery for so long, entices us into yet another obscure and dubious territory. The outcome of her having submitted the declaration to Parliament is not recorded. The copy transcribed here did not come from any Parliamentary archives; it had actually appeared, forty years after it was written, in the possession of the Earl Marschall's family. The next event on record, however, was possibly not unconnected, if not in fact a direct consequence of her intention to fight for some justice. It might best be introduced by the words of the Rev. Douglas Gordon Barron, to whom all subsequent researchers are indebted for his work of collecting and transcribing most of the documents that shed light on the story:

> For some time previous to the Restoration, he [Grainger] had been in failing health ... Doubtless, his decease had been anticipated, but that does not prepare us for the fact that, six months later, his widow, Christian Fletcher, became the wife of James Sandilands, first Lord Abercrombie – a nobleman whose dissolute and worthless life must have contrasted painfully with his whose name and memory she had so rashly hastened to repudiate.

When Barron published *In Defence of the Regalia* in 1910, the series of letters sent by the Countess to Grainger had not yet come to light. Without that pivotal correspondence, it was extremely difficult to account for Grainger's apparently sudden defection, and next to impossible to make any sense of his wife's marriage to the notoriously degenerate Lord Abercrombie.

Abercrombie was about the same age as Christian Fletcher. He had married his first wife, Jean Lichton in 1643. Described by Lamont as a 'riotous youth who spent an old estate in the space of four or five years', Sir James Sandilands was created Lord Abercrombie by Charles I (in Carisbrook) at the end of 1647. Abercrombie's legendary poor management of his money and property was matched by his ability not only to attract scandal in his personal life but to positively promote it. In 1649, he had apparently struck a Church elder and a beadle who had turned up at his door. This was not necessarily, in itself, a bad thing since they had come to insist that his wife appear before the session to answer charges of undisciplined or intemperate sensual behaviour. What is more interesting is the source of this slur on his wife's good name. Abercrombie was called to answer to the Presbytery for the assault and, while they were at it, to answer also for his frequent excesses of drunkenness etc. He subsequently sent in a letter of apology to the Synod of Fife in which he desires that the 'rash and groundless slander' against his lady, first invented by himself, might be referred to the Kirk Session.

Barron's horror at the haste with which the minister's wife had apparently repudiated her husband's name would be no more than a shadow of the effect the news would have had initially, as it spread throughout the parish and beyond. Abercrombie's divorce from Jean Lichton is reported to have taken place on 13 March. On Sunday, 11 October, the week preceding his marriage to Christian Fletcher, he was compearing at Kinneff Kirk in compliance with a summons issued on the 4th, on a charge of fornication (q.v. Supplementary Papers no.11). The name 'Margaret Read' appears to be connected with the charge (although, unfortunately, a part of the document has not survived, so the full text is no longer available). The business was referred to the Presbytery and the following week their judgement was delivered. Again, the problem of the missing area of the page means that there is some uncertainty about the decision but it seems to indicate that an earlier Act of the General Assembly had some bearing on the question and that, consequently he (or they) would not require to be humbled before the congregation. It goes on to say something to the effect that, on production of an extract of the record of his divorce, his marriage to Christian Fletcher can proceed. He appears to have had the document to hand and, accordingly, the marriage was contracted and proclaimed on that same day.

At this point, Christian Fletcher was five-months pregnant. James Grainger had died just before the 20 May and this marriage took place on the 18 October. Her daughter, Margaret, was baptised on 27 February 1664, as the daughter of James Sandilands Lord Abercrombie. In those days, when the most minor indiscretion was brought before the

Kirk session, when the slightest lapse in moral rectitude was universally regarded with righteous alarm, it would be an understatement to say that Christian Fletcher's reputation was ruined and, more significantly, her credibility utterly destroyed. In January 1664, Abercrombie granted his new wife a liferent charter of the estate of Largie.

History is often presented to us as a body of plain, unalterable fact but the truth is we can only tell the story that the available records seem to indicate. At some time in the future, hopefully, the documents will come to light that explain, unequivocally, what took place in these few months. In the absence of hard evidence, we have to draw what inferences we can from the circumstances. 'And no more hand Sir John Keith had in preserving the honours than is here said nor no person else but my husband and I till they were delivered to the Earl of Marschall in Dunnottar.' This is the last line we have from the minister's wife but she certainly did not have the last word. It was a declaration of war on one of the most powerful women in the country, and written by one of the most vulnerable. That her declaration found its way back to the Countess is a fairly safe bet. In the circumstances, the marriage to Abercrombie has all the hallmarks of her having been 'made an offer that she couldn't refuse.' Within two years, Abercrombie was back in financial difficulties.

For the rest of her life, Christian Fletcher was silent on the subject. John Keith's alleged noble service to the Crown was subsequently acknowledged for a second time in 1677 when he was given the title of Earl of Kintore, his patent once again referring to the great service he was believed to have performed in the entire preserving of his Majesty's Royal Honours. Lord Lyon was authorised to grant him an augmentation to his coat of arms of the Crown, Sceptre and Sword.

The bad feeling between Kintore and the Ogilvies flared up again in 1699 when the Earl submitted to Alexander Nisbet his account of the events that had led to the creation of his earldom, for inclusion in Nisbet's forthcoming *System of Heraldry*, a comprehensive catalogue of the arms of Scotland's leading families. Nisbet had also been in touch with George Ogilvy's son, now Sir William, who had submitted his own version of the story and, in spite of the fact that Nisbet was pre-pared to modify the narratives to accommodate both, William Ogilvy had a pamphlet printed (q.v. Supplementary Papers no.14) in which he asserts his parents' leading role in preserving the Honours. This, *The Achievement of George Ogilvy*, was followed by a second pamphlet, *A Clear Vindication and Just Defence for Publishing the Foregoing Account*, and what happened next was a foregone conclusion. The Earl of Kintore raised a libel action (q.v. Supplementary Papers no.21) before the Privy Council, against William Ogilvy and his son David, the details of which, as the Countess would say, are 'too tedious for a letter.' The Ogilvies had not a chance. William Ogilvy was too ill to attend but, in his absence, on 30 July 1702, the Privy Council, of which Kintore was a member, found them both guilty of defamation. David Ogilvy was fined £100 (over £12,000 today) and the pamphlets were ordered to be publicly burned by the hangman.

A week later, a letter was sent to a David Steiven who, acting on Ogilvy's behalf, had seemingly been trying to gather information to support an appeal. He had spoken with Fettercairn schoolteacher, John Gentleman, husband of Margaret Grainger, about the letters from the Countess that her grandparents had kept. He seems to have been una-ware that, as far as the Graingers' descendants were concerned, their family had been betrayed as much by Ogilvy as by the Earl of Kintore. It is probably worth bearing in mind, also, that if Barrass had actually received the full annual pension that was due, the total over the preced-ing forty years (£8,000) would have been worth close to £1,000,000 of today's money.

5 August 1702, Fettercairn – John Gentleman to David Steiven at Catterline.

Sir, – Yours I received last night and in answer thereto, be pleased to know that whatever I said to you concerning the preservation of the Honours is very well known and can be sufficiently proven by letters under the hands of both the Earl of Marschall and his mother, the Countess Marschall, directed to my wife's grandfather and grandmother and, by these letters, it will evidently appear that the Earl of Kintore's name was only borrowed to that affair. And they also declare who were the preservers of the Honours and what methods were taken in preserving the same. But as to your desiring me formally to give it under my hand what passed between the Countess and my wife's grandfather, is that which I am not resolved to do, seeing it may bring me upon a lock and do Barrass no good; it is but a dark kind of a remembering anything I heard that way, and therefore I can not be very positive in rehearsing it again. However if Barrass thinks that he may have any good by seeing these letters, I believe my wife and her sister may let him see them if he will pay sufficiently for the sight of them. This, with my humble duty to Barrass and yourself, is all at present from, – John Gentleman.

Five years later, came the Union of the Parliaments. Almost overnight, 'Scotland's Honours Three' became redundant relics, symbols of a past independence that no one really wanted to talk about; Scotland had moved on. They were locked away in a chest within a bricked-up room in Edinburgh Castle where they were to lie in obscurity for the next 100 years, almost a fitting metaphor for Christian Fletcher's memory. The Regalia were eventually unearthed again thanks mainly to the efforts of Sir Walter Scott. But the story of the minister's wife, although touched upon by Scott and many others over the years, was always fraught too much with contradiction to be brought into the light.

The last document in archive to mention her name was written in 1737. It concerns Christian Granger, widow of Thomas Gentleman, and the sister of Margaret Grainger who was married to John Gentleman. The sisters were daughters of the Graingers' eldest son, the Rev. John Grainger.

Memorial for Christian Granger, relict of Thomas Gentleman, vintner in Dundee, and their daughter, humbly offered to the consideration of the right honourable the barons of his Majesty's Exchequer.

Christian Fletcher, spouse to Mr James Granger, minister of Kinneff, and grandmother to the said Christian Granger, having been very instrumental in preserving the Regalia of Scotland during the time of the grand rebellion, upon the Restoration, an act of Parliament was made in her favour appointing 2,000 merks to be paid her by his Majesty's Treasurer out of the readiest of his Majesty's rents as a testimony of the Parliament's sense before and therein mentioned, a copy of which act, taken from the extract ready to be shown, is herewith produced, but the money was never paid her.

The said Christian Granger is grandchild to the above Christian Fletcher as appears by the declaration of honest people, a copy whereof is herewith produced and the principal ready to be shown. The memorialist, Christian Granger, was married to the said Thomas Gentleman, and for some years had a comfortable enough subsistence, during which time she never made any attempt for payment of the said sum; but now that her husband is dead and has left his affairs in great disorder, she and her daughter are reduced to great straits and thereby rendered fit objects of compassion and charity, which, joined to their right in virtue of the foresaid act of Parliament, sufficiently entitles them to the benefit of his Majesty's bounty, and its humbly hoped the honourable Barons of his Majesty's Exchequer will put them upon the charity roll for such sum yearly during their joint lives as to them in their great goodness and wisdom shall think meet and proper; and the memorialists will ever pray.

Thanks to the Kinneff Old Church Preservation Trust, the small Kirk of Kinneff, home of Scotland's Regalia for nearly nine years, still stands as a quaint and intriguing monument to early Presbyterianism and, of course, to James Grainger. But even there, in that modest, reassuring temple of truth, the minister's wife seems almost to be an embarrassment to an otherwise romantic story. A large stone plaque on one wall remembers George Ogilvy's deeds and pride of place goes to the nineteenth-century Grainger memorial, crafted in stone with its gilded and painted Crown, Sceptre and Sword surmounting a section of James Grainger's original gravestone. Loosely translated from the original Latin, the poetic Victorian inscription reads:

Behold the spot where Grainger's ashes lie who, from besieged Dunnottar, safe conveyed the insignia of Scotland's Royalty and in this hallowed ground in secret laid, where now he rests himself, Heaven shall bestow meet recompense and such desert as his. He, who his country's honour saved below, now wields a sceptre in the realms of bliss.

It could not have occurred to the writers of this epitaph that the slight on the minister's wife was equally an insult to Grainger's memory but, clearly, the marriage to Abercrombie had served its purpose and more. The perverse human capacity to believe the worst of the best of people while believing only the best of the worst was amply exhibited, as it had been ably exploited.

It wasn't just James Grainger's bones that had been laid to rest in the Kinneff churchyard; the truth − Christian Fletcher's story − had been well and truly buried along with them. She died in February 1691, at the age of seventy-one − a name all but forgotten in Scottish history.

Supplementary Papers

I – CROMWELL TO THE COMMITTEE OF ESTATES.

9 October 1650, Linlithgow.
For the Right Honourable the Committee of Estates of Scotland,
at Stirling or elsewhere.

My Lords, – the grounds and ends of the army's entering Scotland, have been heretofore often and clearly made known unto you, and how much we have desired the same might be accomplished without blood. But, according to what returns we have received, it is evident your hearts had not that love to us as we can truly say we had towards you. And we are persuaded these difficulties in which you have involved yourselves by espousing your King's interest, and taking into your bosom that person in whom, (notwithstanding what has or may be said to the contrary), that which is really malignancy and all malignants do centre, against whose family the Lord has so eminently withstood for blood guiltiness, nor to be done away with such superficial and formal shows of repentance as are expressed in his late declaration; and your strange prejudice against us as men of heretical opinions, (which, through the great goodness of God to us, have been unjustly charged upon us), have occasioned your rejecting of those overtures which, with a Christian affection, we offered to you before any blood was spilt, or your people had suffered damage by us.

The daily sense we have of the calamity of war laying upon the poor people of this nation, and the sad consequences of blood and famine likely to come upon him; the advantages given to malignants, profane and popish party by this war; and that reality of affection which we have so often professed to you, and concerning the truth of which, we have so solemnly appealed, does again constrain us to send unto you, to let you know that, if the contending for that person be not by you preferred to the peace and welfare of our country, the blood of your people, the love of men of the same faith with you, and which is above all, the honour of that God we serve; then give the state of England that satisfaction and security for the peaceable and quiet living by you that may, in justice, be demanded from a nation giving so just a ground to ask the same from those who have, as you, taken their enemy unto their bosom, whilst he was in hostility against them; and it will be made good to you that you may have a lasting and durable peace with them, and the wish of a blessing upon you in all religious and civil things.

If this be refused by you, we are persuaded that God, who has born his testimony, will do it again on behalf of his poor servants, who do appeal to him whether these desires flow from sincerity of heart or not. I rest, your Lordship's humble servant, – O. Cromwell.

2 – OGILVY TO LOUDON, 1651.

Some documents are all the more interesting when presented after the story has been told. In this, in October 1651, while the Committee of Estates were anxious about the security of the Regalia, George Ogilvy is writing to the Earl of Loudon:

George Ogilvy – For the Rt. Hon the Earl of Loudon, Lord High Chancellor of Scotland.

My Lord, – Having been sundry times pressed to deliver the honours, as first by my Lord Callendar, by an order of the Committee of Estates sitting in Aberdeen, and thereafter by the Lord Balcarras, by a order by the same committee and last of all, by a letter from the Lord Balcarras to me to deliver the honours to Sir Arthur Forbes, grounded upon a letter from your Lordship and the rest of the Committee of Estates of the tenth of September last, all which orders they may conceive to have been sufficient for them to have received the honours, but as I conceive no sufficient warrant for me to deliver them, having received the charge of that house and what was entrusted therein from the Earl Marschall and then by a particular warrant under his Majesty's own hand.

Yet, notwithstanding, if your Lordship and the Committee of Estates shall conceive that they may be more secure in any other place than they are here, I shall deliver them to whom your Lordship and the Committee of Estates shall appoint to receive them, they bringing with them an Act of the Committee for the Earl Marschall and my exoneration thereof, and that I have, additionally, a particular order for the delivery of them, but moreover, humbly submitting to your Lordship's and Committee of Estates' better consideration, I conceive that there is no place in this kingdom where they can be more secure, than where they are, and with less charges, if the Committee of Estates be pleased to take order timeously for furnishing me with such things as are necessary for the defence of this house – for all former orders that were appointed for the furnishing of it are altogether disobeyed; where the general commissary should have sent in six hundred bols of meal I have not received the half thereof and, as I am credibly informed he has sold and is selling the rest of it in Aberdeen, and for the maintenance of the Mearns, which was appointed for this house, you will find the heritors' answer by the copy of a letter to me from the clerk of the Committee of the Shire here enclosed – I humbly desire that the Committee of Estates would be pleased to give order that I may have a hundred men appointed for the defence the house of which as yet I have received but forty.

I have sent your Lordship the double of my letter to the Lord Balcarras whereby my proceedings may be known. If he be there, you will be pleased to let him have it for I have sent one of purpose with it to the chancelry of Ross, for Sir Arthur Forbes would not, upon any terms, undertake to send my answer to the Lord Balcarras, although the Committee of Estates, in the letter to the Lord Balcarras did speak as well of the King's stuff as of the Honours yet neither in his letter to me nor in his order to Sir Arthur Forbes was it so much as mentioned and I hope that if you resolve to remove the Honours you will think upon some course for his Majesty's stuff.

If it would please the Committee of Estates to liberate the Earl Marschall's and his mother's lands in Buchan, Mar and Mearns from the Marquis of Huntly and appoint them for the garrison of this house, there will be as many men as I shall desire for the defence of the same, all of which I humbly remit to the wise consideration of the Committee of Estates and that they may be pleased to let me know their resolutions herein that I may the better dispose of the affairs concerning this house and that your Lordship pardon the tediousness of this letter which I could not shorten in respect that the business therein is of so high a concern, these I humbly entreat may be imparted to the Committee of Estates from, your Lordship's most humble servant, – George Ogilvy.

3 – KING TO OGILVY, 1652.

The King, up until the time of the capitulation of Dunnottar, had hoped to get supplies to the castle by ship, while also removing the Regalia, together with some valuable possessions held there. He badly needed the revenue that might have been raised from the sale of some of his silver and plate but, in the end, probably through lack of funds, the project took too long to organise. The idea was finally abandoned in June, by which time the Cromwellians were already in possession of Dunnottar. In this next, written in April, the King is promising help if Ogilvy can hold out until winter. John Keith, incidentally, had left Dunnottar at the beginning of February 1652 carrying Ogilvy's letter to the King. He finally arrived at Paris on 11 April. This letter, which had remained amongst the King's papers, appears to have been intended to be presented to Ogilvy by the proposed commander of the expedition, Major General Vandruscke.

> The King, to Our trusty and welbeloved the Governor of our Castle of Dunnottar.
>
> Trusty and welbeloved, we greet you well. Your letter of the first of February came not to our hands till yesterday, the messenger who

brought it having met with several ill accidents in his journey, and we cannot at present better express the high value and esteem we have of your singular fidelity and merit towards us, than by making this haste in dispatching the bearer General Major Vandruscke to you with the return of our gracious acceptation and hearty thanks for the great service you have done us, in preserving that important castle for us, which we doubt not in the end will contribute as well to the benefit and advantage of that our ancient Kingdom, as to your particular reputation and honour. We wish that other men who were entrusted by us with the custody of palaces as defensible as that is, had given the same instances of affection to us, and courage as you have done, in condemning such rebellious summons, which would have made it much easier for us to have redeemed our good subjects of that our kingdom from the present oppression and slavery they live under, for the doing whereof that place preserved by your faithfulness must be now the only foundation. You shall assure all the officers, gentlemen and soldiers who are with you, and are resolute to stand by you in this good and great service, that we have a just sense of their affections, and hope to live to be able liberally to gratify and reward them.

In the meantime, we shall not fail to use all possible means for their relief, in such a manner as the season of the year, and the power of the rebels at sea will permit. And if you shall be able to defend and keep the place till the beginning of the next winter (which we hope you will do), we make no question but that we shall transport such supplies to you as shall not only be sufficient to enlarge your quarters, but by the blessing of God, to free your country from the tyranny of these rebels. We desire to receive as frequent information from you as is possible of the true state of our affairs in that our kingdom, and your own particular condition, and such advice upon the whole, as either upon your own observation and experience, or upon intelligence with such other of our good subjects who preserve their affections entire to us, however they are for the present compelled to submit to the prevailing power, you think fit to send to us and that you continue a constant correspondence with Lieutenant General Middleton, through whose hands you shall receive directions

from us upon all occasions. And so we bid you very hearty farewell. –
Given at the Louvre in Paris this 12th day of April 1652.

4 – OGILVIES OF BALFOUR AND SCHANNALIE TO BARRASS, 1660.

In the scramble for recognition after the Restoration, George Ogilvy, not being *au fait* with the way these things are done, was slow to seize his opportunity. In the following two letters to him, written at the time of his petition being presented, his relatives express their frustration with his failure to properly tend his own interests:

28 September 1660, Purrie – John Ogilvy of Balfour to George Ogilvy of Barrass.

Much honoured cousin, I have been long by the way and falling sick in Kirkaldy so you could not hear sooner from me, I doubt not but your son has acquainted you how it has gone in relation to your business, but to be short with you, I do not think that my Lord Marschall ever mentioned your name in relation to the Honours of Scotland but has past all in his brother John's name who is made Knight Marschall and has four hundred pound sterling a year conferred on him and inserted in his patent that the honour and pension is given him for preserving the Crown and Sceptre of Scotland.

So you may judge whether it had not been better for you to have followed friends' advice and gone up yourself. I had done what was fitting, in your absence, before leaving London, both in recommending your son to my Lord Ogilvy [Airly] and a great many other friends. My Lord did present your son to his Majesty and likewise acquainted him with your business, how you had preserved and still had these honours, now it only rests on you to bestir yourself, for it is not something of small moment to be neglected and, if you have not delivered them as yet, I think it absolutely fitting you do not deliver them to my Lord Marschall at all, but take some speedy course to mend what you have neglected. So hoping you will take this to consideration since it concerns your credit so much. I shall need say no more but shall be ready to meet or speak with you where you please and both in that and anything else shall strive to witness myself Your real cousin to serve you, J. Ogilvy.

29 *September 1660 – James Ogilvy of Schannalie to George Ogilvy of Barrass.*

Much honoured and loving brother, what I would say to you, at such a distance, I cannot entrust to paper, only this far, counsel is no command and whatever your lazy or peevish neglect of a matter of so great consequence both in relation to honour advancement and a constant heritable fortune for you and all yours in all succeeding ages has produced, you may be sensible of your own part and of the wholesome, seasonable (if than received) counsel and advise of your faithful and real friends and myself in particular, how pressingly, affectionately, (and during our abode last together) incessantly I entreated, exhorted and brotherly advised you to wean all affairs and in proper person to agent your own business at London. And at our last parting in Killimur, you promised, with all convenience, I should hear from you, whereupon I retarded my brother's journey much of a month.

But you thought so little of our advice and slighted the business of so high concern that we never had a line from you neither did your son look upon us so much as to salute his friends by the way. What the result can or shall be to you is uncertain, merely depending upon your own consideration. If you intend to pass from your compearance and suffer and see another man enjoy the fruits, honour and profit of your labours, we must rest satisfied. But for my own part, my respects are so to you that I wish from my heart I had gifted you a hundred pieces to have been your charges and made my own expenses to attend you back and forth, if this had been needful, but in the contrary, if your peevish nature could have allowed you, (blessed be God) you stand in need of no mans supply, and my brother was ready and willing, upon his own charges, to have waited upon you and to have done you all the good offices that lay in his power, and at London (as he told me) the business is fairly forward and you have many friends.

So it rests that you bestir yourself one way or other and, upon advertisement, my brother and I shall wait upon you and he will be able to give you a more ample account than this expostulatory letter of mine and shall only add that I wish to secure the honours and, if it be possible, that you would convey them to your friends where they may be for your use in better security than any part in the Mearns. It would appear you must either quit my Lord Marschall or your interest in this. You have to choose. If I were in your place I know what I would do, and in the meantime you may believe that I am, Your real, faithful brother and ready servant, − J. Ogilvy

5 − WILLIAM OGILVY TO HIS FATHER.

It was October 1660 before James Grainger heard that Ogilvy's son, William, was in London. In her reply to Grainger of 14 October 1660, the Countess writes: 'Indeed for his son's petitioning for him at London, we were informed of that before, by a letter from his son to him, which my son, I believe, has acquainted him with, since the honours were received.' The following, written by William Ogilvy, seems to be the letter the Countess refers to in this curious and oddly candid admission:

15 September 1660 – Westminster, in Stephens Alley, at Mr Axtillis House.

Loving father, since my last to you I have made little progress on account of the Duke of Gloucester's death and the arrival of the Spanish ambassador which have so troubled the King that none, for this eight days, dare move any business to his Majesty till he be a little appeased and till some days of mourning be past. But I am confident that the business about the Honours, which the King knows of at length, shall go very well, provided you keep them undelivered till a new order comes to you and, I hope, a new pension or some other commodity besides honour with it. So if it were your pleasure to come this length yourself, it would be well worth your pains; and if you cannot come yourself, write to the King and write your mind to me what you would have done, for we cannot go back with what we have already motioned and have very good hopes of, and especially the best of our friends being engaged in the business.

For when I saw at first that the business was going wrong here, I wrote my friends that you had sent me to represent you, as I have and shall, God willing, continue to do especially in this business wherein, if it be rightly managed, I hope all that shall succeed us shall have credit for it; for all our countrymen look so much upon it that they say there is no Scotsman here can say the like, and the King will not let you want a liberal reward for it.

So keep them till I acquaint you upon any condition. And if my Lord Marschall has surprised you with the King's order before my letter came into your hands, you must either come or write to the King that you had them and that you and your wife have suffered for them, and preserved them till this time that you have obeyed his Majesty's order. And if you have got a receipt for them, you must send it to me that I may show it. But it would be better if you kept them till I acquaint you. For I assure you that your name was never heard in the business till I came, and I hope you will consider the more of it and will not abide from this, seeing your best friends and I both are engaged to the King to make it good that you were the only preserver of these Honours under God.

I shall haste through business as soon as I can, but I have got a strange trick played on me which is thus: Colonel J. Ogilvy had a study in his chamber and I had none in mine so he desired me to put in my portmanteau in his closet for security, which I did, with all my money in it. Within five days after his going home, the Duke of Gloucester died and the Court went into mourning. I went to count my money, to see what I had, and worked out what I had spent, and I found I was missing fifteen pounds sterling. I tried my man and the maid, and all that were in the house, for my money. They swore they handled it not, for none had the key of the closet but the Colonel's man, a young tailor who had come up to serve him for a time and to see and learn the fashions. He made my clothes and, when he made them, he had not so much money as to buy candle to sow them by until I gave it to him, as the Colonel knows, but, when he went away, he let the maid see a length of excellent cloth worth twenty shillings a yard, with accessories and many other things for women that he had bought, and he told her he was taking them to France with him.

So, by all probability, he stole the money. I desire you to write to the Colonel to search for him and to put him to a trial, and I doubt not but that he will be found guilty. I would not need much had this not happened, but you must supply me with some now, for I can get none here upon any terms ...

6 – BARRASS'S ASSERTIONS ANSWERED.

While William Ogilvy was in London, on his father's behalf, efforts to put a stop to his father's 'pretensions' were gaining momentum. Dated 8 November 1660, this appears to have been a draft of a document intended, ultimately, to block Ogilvy's petition. It does not appear to have been written by the Countess; it seems to be missing her turn of phrase. It is quite interesting, nonetheless, especially if it is John Keith's work. In this, Ogilvy is being blamed for 'burdening my Lord Marshall's brother by his declaring to the English that he had carried them away, which banished him for about 3 years.' Forty years later, in the Proceedings of the Privy Council, the story has become: 'Sir George and his wife ... asserted the Honours were carried abroad by the pursuer [John Keith], and delivered to the King at Paris, which was indeed the contrivance that the pursuer then advised, and the principal cause of his going abroad.'

This document was included in 'Papers relative to the preservation of the Honours of Scotland, in Dunnottar Castle, 1651–1652.' Edited by Charles R.A. Howden, the Scottish History Society, Vol. 26.

Whereas George Ogilvy makes several assertions in reference to his part in preserving the Honours of Scotland. Therefore the truth is declared in the ensuing answers.

1. He affirms that always since Mr James Grainger had them first in his custody, he has had his oath never to deliver them to any person whatsoever but unto him.

Answer: About the time of his Majesty's arrival in England, George Ogilvy had occasion to be with my Lady Marshall, at which time she told him that she being certain that how soon his Majesty minded these honours, and resolved to commit them to convenient keeping, there would come some order or direction to her to deliver them to any should be entrusted. Therefore she intended (as conceiving it most pertinent) to remove them from Mr Granger's house unto her own dwelling. But she promised to advertise him before she removed them. His answer was in no way negative but gave his opinion that she needed not be too sudden till his Majesty was well settled.

According her promise, one day or two before she intended to send for them by a letter, she advertised George Ogilvy, which how soon he received, he went straight to Mr Grainger's house and, finding him in bed, in a chamber alone, he went in and, bolting the door behind him, he told him, there was a business which most nearly concerned him and wherein, if the minister helped him not, he was for evermore ruined, and it was within the compass of his power to preveine the danger or not; and therefore showed him there was a necessity of his promise to help him to his power, by which words and the like he preingaged Mr Grainger by his solemn promise, and then told him it was not to deliver the Honours unto any without his consent. But the next day my Lady Marshall sending for them, the minister perceived himself circumveined, and much resented his simplicity.

2. That when the Committee sent their order to Mr Grainger to deliver the Honours to Balmaine [Gilbert Ramsey] and James Peadie, and they to deliver them to Whiteriggs that Mr Grainger offered willingly unto him

the whole Honours so to preveine the Council's order, but that he would not take them at that time, wanting conveniency to carry them, except only the sceptre; but gave him his receipt on all, and took the minister's ticket to deliver him the rest when he desired.

Answer: George Ogilvy having notice of this order of the Committee, and finding himself slighted therein, represented to the minister that the obeying of that order would tend absolutely to both their prejudices (although the Committee, in their order, had thanked Mr Granger, and promised him reward), and advised him to give the Honours unto him before the order came, and then should he be free from obeying it. The minister answered he would not, nor would not be any more deceived by his unhandsome policy.

But while they thus debating, there comes a servant of Whiteriggs with a letter in relation to the order, at which George Ogilvy took occasion to entreat the minister to do something presently that so he might have something of a ground to answer the Sheriff. And if he would not give him all, let him have but the sceptre and he should give him the receipt of all which he might show, to testify he had delivered all, to which the minister condescended upon George Ogilvy's great oath to restore it whensoever he called for it. And the minister gave George Ogilvy a ticket testifying that though George Ogilvy had given a receipt for the whole, yet he had received but the Sceptre.

Moreover when my Lord Marshall sent, from Bolshan, his depute and Arthur Straton of Snadown, with the Kings letter to my Lady to deliver them to her son, and her letter to Mr Grainger to deliver them to these in her son's name, Mr Grainger went to Barrass requiring from him the Sceptre, the Kings order being come to deliver the Honours. Notwithstanding of his former oath, he absolutely refused to give it, so that these messengers returned without having received them because they would not take one part without the other.

3. That Mr James Grainger went unanimously with him to Dunnottar to deliver the Honours.

Answer: My Lord Marschall having given a precept to Mr Grainger, and an
express command to Barrass, to bring in to Dunnottar on Monday the
8th October, each of them, that part of the Honours which they had,
George Ogilvy wrote to Mr Grainger to come to his house at Craigie,
with the Crown and Sword, and that to the effect they might go jointly
together, and deliver all, the minister answered that he scorned to come
to his house, nor would he have more to do with him in that nor in anything else; but that seeing he had perjured himself in refusing to return
him the Sceptre, he would go alone and deliver the rest by himself. Yet,
notwithstanding of this answer, George Ogilvy to take away any seeming
of difference between them in the delivery, met the minister upon the
road and so went on with him to Dunnottar

4. That he was most affectionately received by my Lord into Dunnottar yea
even unto embracing.

Answer: The minister and he having brought in the Honours all at one
time, notice was given to my Lord, who directed to bring them into
a room and having looked upon the Honours, he thanked them both
in general, though more particularly the minister, and commanded the
sheriff depute (to whom he had given the charge of the house) to lift
the Crown and carry it to a closet. George Ogilvy being moved thereat,
snatched at the Sceptre and carried it in undesired, and a certain space
thereafter tarried in the dining room with the rest of those then attend-
ing, but received nothing afterward from the Lord but downlooking and
frowns. And the next morning my Lord caused my Lord Arbuthnott send
him word that my Lord absolutely discharged him from any more seeing
his face, which he has not since.

5. That he alone has been the only sufferer, loser, and person endangered for
the preserving of these Honours.

Answer: The time he was prisoner (which was the whole sum of his suffering) he liberated himself from all suffering, loss or danger, by burdening

my Lord Marshall's brother by his declaring to the English that he had carried them away, which banished him for about 3 years, which time he was exposed to both hazard and want, being robbed in his travelling, my Lady, his mother at great expenses for him, and his bills of exchange miscarried, himself in several hazards of taking before he could land and reach the hills of Scotland where General Middleton was in arms and when all got then capitulations, his was hardly obtained but by much mediation. Also Mr Grainger's wife was not without much hazard in conveying them through many of the English between Dunnottar and her own house.

6. Where he avers that my Lord Marschall, with good will and favour, has given him a receipt of purpose to witness that they have been in his custody ever since they were first put into Dunnottar, and also to testify that he has now received them completely from him.

Answer: It is evidently clear that my Lord Marshall being fully assured (and it being the thing that Barrass in his foresaid assertions dare not deny) that from the day these Honours were carried out of Dunnottar until the 8th of the last October, which day they were delivered to my Lord Marshall, they were constantly in Mr Grainger's particular custody and likewise the major part of them being personally delivered by Mr Grainger, that part which Barrass delivered being cunningly wrested and perjuredly retained for about eight days from the man that had preserved it with the rest to that day.

I say, therefore, it is clear that receipt has not been given of purpose to testify they had been always in George Ogilvy's keeping, or that they were received entirely from him, but the reasons moving my Lord Marshall to grant that receipt, and which those who were solicitors for Barrass to that effect, have pressed in upon him are:

Because they were in Dunnottar when Barrass was put into it;

Because Barrass was charged with them by my Lord's mother;

Because he presumed having the sceptre, to retain it till he got some acknowledgement by way of receipt; and,

Because William Ogilvies petition was answered with a command to deliver them, and take a receipt thereon, which they have interpret to my Lord Marshall as a command on him to give one.

[These next seemingly revised points were appended.]

That they were in Dunnottar when Barrass was put in;

That he had an immediate charge from my Lady Marshall to secure them by putting them out of house;

That, afterwards, he did once or twice visit them and helped Mr Grainger to shift them from one place to another;

That he and his wife were prisoners in Aberdeen and Dunnottar till they produced Mr John Keith's receipt;

Is all true, and all that he can truly allege.

But all the foresaid assertions, or that he had power to remove them from Mr Grainger without my Lady Marshall's warrant are arrogant untruths.

7 – GEORGE OGILVY'S PETITION.

The following was sent to James Grainger either with or shortly after the Countess's letter of 14 October, i.e. towards the end of the time in which Grainger believed Ogilvy was the only one who was trying, for personal gain, to claim credit for the preservation of the Regalia. Ironically, in this extended period of co-operation with the Countess, his antipathy towards Ogilvy is a measure of the minister's outrage that anyone should think to benefit from an act of mere duty to his King. It is hard not to admire the craft and the audacity of Marie Erskine who, knowing her own son already has his title and pension and that it is only a matter of time before Grainger finds out, can still manipulate the minister through his righteousness. A copy of Ogilvy's petition, having somehow found its way into the Countess's hands, she sent it to Grainger, clearly with the invitation to study it and to comment on its veracity.

To the Kings most Excellent Majesty, the Humble Petition of George Ogilvy of Barrass in your Majesty's kingdom of Scotland, Showeth,

That your petitioner during the late troubles in the said kingdom and in time of greatest danger and extremity did, according to the trust reposed in him by the Earl Marshall there, secure your Majesty's crown, sword and sceptre, being the honours of that ancient kingdom, for which his faithful service and loyalty your petitioner has suffered highly both in his person and estate through the envy and malice of disaffected persons who shut up both your petitioner and his wife close prisoners in the Castle of Dunnottar by the space of a whole year together, not allowing them, in all that time, the freedom of a servant to attend them, (the grief of which imprisonment, together with their cruel usage and threatening, quickly after broke the heart of your petitioner's said wife and occasioned her death), being continually terrified with tortures and torments, and threatened to have both their lives and fortunes taken from them. And finding all their threatening and terrors could nowise prevail, at last they proffered your petitioner great sums of money for the said honours, which your petitioner, notwithstanding all his sufferings and necessities, could never be induced to entertain at so dear a rate as the forfaulture of his loyalty.

Whereupon after much hardship and vexation your petitioner and his said deceased wife were enlarged upon bail of £2,000 sterling, to re-enter prison upon demand. But, notwithstanding this enlargement, your petitioners house was frequently searched for the said honours, in so much that he durst never venture to bring them home, but was necessitate to entrust them with Mr James Grainger, an honest minister of your petitioners own parish, under his oath of secrecy and assurance to redeliver the same unto your petitioner whensoever he should be thereunto required, which accordingly he did perform, neither he nor any body else save your petitioner being ever questioned for the same.

That at length by your Majesty's special order, your petitioner was enjoined to deliver up the said honours unto the said Earl Marshall, which your petitioner (in obedience to your Majesty's commands) did readily and willingly obey, as by the acquittance of the said Earl (written word by word with his own hand), which was by your petitioner lately presented to and perused by your royal Majesty, more at large may appear, an exact duplicate of which said acquittance is hereunto annexed. May it please your sovereign Majesty in tender consideration of your petitioners said service and sufferings to confer upon him and his posterity such a mark of honour whereby your Majesty's favour and gracious acceptance of his integrity and loyalty may be transmitted to the memory of succeeding generations, that so both your petitioner and others, being encouraged by this example of your Majesty's royal bounty, may with the more zeal and alacrity expose themselves to all future adventures for the honour and preservation of your Majesty's crown and Kingdome, and that your Majesty would likewise graciously settle upon the petitioner such an annuity or other casuality as your Majesty shall think.

8 – GRAINGER'S CRITIQUE OF OGILVY'S PETITION, 1661.

On 16 October, the Countess writing to Grainger, says: '… how soon you have leisure to draw up that paper you may be pleased to send it, that I may see it. I believe neither you nor I aim at anything but to clear truth, and discover that man's untruths.' James Grainger obliged with the following critique of Ogilvy's petition, sent to the Countess some time between 16 and 28 October 1661:

Ane Extract of some untruths from a petition entitled 'To the King's Most Excellent Majesty, the Humble Petition of George Ogilvy of Barras' (By Mr James Grainger).

Since it has pleased God amongst others to make me instrumental in the preservation of the Honours of the kingdom, I cannot but testify against the impudence of those who assume unto themselves that they were the only preservers of the same, and especially against this petition made up of so many untruths.

For the first, the petitioner says, in the beginning of the petition, that the Honours were entrusted to him by the Earl Marschall, but the Earl

Marschall gave him no trust of that room where the honours lay, it being his cabinet, for his Lordship kept the key thereof himself until he was taken captive at Eliot [Alyth] and taken aboard ship. Then his Lordship sent forth the key with Whiteriggs who brought it to my Lord's mother, the Countess of Marschall, who speedily thereafter did horse and come to Dunnottar and took forth the Honours out of the cabinet and delivered them to the petitioner with a charge that he should be careful to secure them.

Secondly, he says he did secure them, but he was so far from securing them that he put them in great hazard by keeping them unsecured, although he had been often, both by me and others, advised to the contrary; and when he had resolved to secure them, perceiving them to be in great hazard, he was at his wits end and knew not what to do, but Providence directs him to me and he will entrust them to me, if I would take in hand to secure them, which, when I had condescended unto, he knew not nor could devise the way how to bring them secretly to my hand. But I, not being in health myself, behoved to devise all and caused my wife put in execution what I devised and bring them forth and then I secured them.

A third untruth: he says that he and his wife were shut up close prisoners a whole year together, whereas the whole space he abode there as a prisoner was only ten months and, of that time, he was not close prisoner much above the space of a month and then the liberty of the whole bounds of the castle was granted to them.

Fourthly, whereas it is said that during the whole space of their imprisonment, they had not the liberty of a servant, this liberty was denied them only for the space of a month and then they had one, James Ogilvy, to serve them, whom they made choice of themselves.

Fifthly, whereas it is said that {the said imprisonment broke his wife's heart and occasioned her death} [the words within the curly brackets are scored out] his house was often searched for the honours, the like was never heard in the parish where he dwells, and I think the usurpers themselves did never suspect them to be there and so could not search his house for them.

Sixthly, whereas it is said in the petition that he was necessitate to entrust them to Mr James Grainger under his oath of secrecy and assurance to redeliver the same when he should be required; I wonder how a man professing himself to be a Christian could make so bold to vent such untruths, especially to a king. But what will not covetousness and ambition enforce their slaves to do; and to have these richly served is the end of this petition, as the close of it shows.

But to come to the untruths vented here, – first, he says he delivered them to me but it was his wife that delivered them to my wife. Then he says he delivered them to me under oath of secrecy and assurance to redeliver them. He never sought any such thing of me, neither could he, at that time, for I saw him not after the honours came to my hand till the castle was surrendered. I spoke with him, indeed, before the sword was delivered for I behoved to go to Dunnottar in a boat, not being able to travel neither on foot nor horse, and devise the way how to bring forth the sword, and then all of us gave an oath of secrecy, and no more than this was ever sought excepting only that he desired me, as soon as health would permit, that I should go to the Countess of Marschall and show her ladyship so much, which I did and set it down under my hand where I had laid them; yet he says I did accordingly perform the same. This is a known untruth for he deceitfully got the sceptre from me two days before I delivered the honours and as deceitfully came to my Lord Marschall before I saw him and obtained a ticket of receipt as if he had all to deliver. But my Lord Marschall's letter to me and his also written the day before they were delivered will prove that he was not the deliverer of the same.

And, besides this, when we had brought in the honours to Dunnottar, we were sent with them to a chamber till my Lord Marschall should come to us and receive them and, having laid them down upon a table in the chamber, as soon as my Lord Marschall came in, I took them up, one by one, and delivered them into his Lordship's hand, before many witnesses. This was on the eighth of October 1660, having kept them from February in the year 1652 until that day.

In the petition, he says I did accordingly perform what I had given him assurance of in redelivering them to him. This is the most notable untruth, for they continued constantly in my custody until the day that, according to his Majesty's command in a letter to the Countess of Marschall to deliver them to her son, I did deliver them to my Lord Marschall in Dunnottar Castle before many famous witnesses, of which my Lord Arbuthnott and the before-written Sheriff-Depute were two, I having kept them entire near the space of nine years. Only two or three days before the said delivery, Barrass, by a lying policy, to prevent the Council's order, got the sceptre upon his solemn oath that he should not deceive me. I, thinking that he was obliged by that oath to restore it to me, sought the sceptre again but he refused that he had sworn any such thing ...

Whereas it may be clearly seen that he sought the sceptre from me and kept it up that he might pretend a hand in the delivery of them, by which pretence, he deceitfully purchased a receipt on the whole honours from the Earl Marschall upon which receipt he grounded his lying petition, although the Earl Marschall's own letter and another from Barrass to me written and sent to me the day before the honours were delivered will testify that none but I either had them or delivered them.

9 – COUNTESS'S EDITED VERSION OF GRAINGER'S CRITIQUE.

The Countess's amended version of the above was sent to James Grainger on 28 October along with her letter in which she writes:

I here send you my thoughts of the paper you sent me, whose substance is the same with yours, only I conceive this to be the best way in answering his untruths particularly; but you may mend what you find amiss or not well-worded, and when you think it right, you will write it over your self and set your name to it.

The Countess does not seem to have materially altered the document. It is a bit more concise and she added a touch of her characteristic poetic alliteration: '... he did nothing either in contrivance or conveyance', but, altogether, she seems to have been quite pleased with Grainger's work, as well she might.

'An Answer to some untruths extracted from are petition entitled: To the Kings most Excellent Majesty, the humble Petition of George Ogilvy of Barrass.' (Amended version.)

Since it has pleased God amongst others to make me instrumental in the preservation of the honours of the kingdom, I cannot but testify against the impudence of those who assume unto themselves that they were the only preservers of the same, and especially against this petition made up of so many untruths.

For first, the petitioner says in the beginning of his petition, that the honours were entrusted to him by the Earl Marshall. So far was he from being entrusted with the honours that, during the whole time the house was maintained, he never had access to the closet in which they were laid up, but the key thereof was exactly kept by the Earl himself until he was made prisoner and on shipboard; at which time he sent the key privately to the Countess, his mother, by Robert Keith, sheriff Depute of the Mearns desiring her to go presently to Dunnottar, and take course for preserving of the honours. And so accordingly with all diligence she went. But because of the enemy's sudden approach they could not be brought safely out of the Castle. Therefore she delivered them unto Barrass, charging him that whether he should be necessitate to capitulate or not, he should secure them from all danger. So that all the trust he had was only from the Earl's mother.

2. That he only did secure them:

His part therein was so small that instead of securing them he had almost (by long delay) brought them to the point of losing. For, not-withstanding he suspected that necessity would force a surrender of the castle, and also being often advised, both by myself and others, to dispose of the honours in time, yet he always deferred the same till the house was in hazard when, being at his wits end, Providence directed him to me; and, when I had undertaken to secure them, he could not contrive which way to convey them to my hand, so that I behoved to devise the way myself, and caused my wife put in execution what I myself could not do undetected.

3. That he and his wife were shut up close prisoners for a whole year, not having all that time the liberty of a servant:

The whole space of their imprisonment was not fully ten months; nor were they kept in close prison but a month, or little more, having the liberty of all Dunnottar Castle the rest of that time, with a servant of their own choosing to attend them, by name James Ogilvy.

4. That his house was frequently searched for them:

It is known to all then living thereabout, that his house was never searched for them, for there was no particular place any more suspected from the time the Earl Marschall's brother John's receipt was produced by Barrass to General Major Deane and other officers.

5. That he was necessitate to entrust them to Mr James Grainger under his oath of secrecy:

He never sought of me a particular oath of secrecy. For they being once in my custody I had more need of his oath then he had of mine, and therefore a mutual oath was past amongst us all for keeping secret. But where he insinuates that all I did was but in discharge of my trust to him, I declare that, of all the hands that were helpful in the business, his was the least, for he did nothing either in contrivance or conveyance, save only that his wife delivered the honours unto mine.

6. That I gave him assurance to redeliver them unto him whensoever he should require them:

No assurance nor other engagement whatsoever thereto relating was ever required by him or given by me, he being glad they were fallen in my hand whose honesty he had formerly experimented. Only he desired that, with all conveniency, I should go to the Countess of Marschall and make known to her all the procedure, (himself also signifying her by letter that, if she thought them not secure enough in my hand, she might do with them as she thought fit). This desire I obeyed, and delivered unto my Lady a ticket under my hand, specifying the particular place in which they were secured, that so upon all occasions she might know where to find them.

1 Dunnottar Castle from the main adjacent high ground

2 The lower part of the path leading to the castle

Left: 3 Gun loop-holes in the outside wall

Below left: 4 The tunnel entrance viewed from the portcullis

Opposite above: 5 Tunnel leading to the plateau

Opposite below: 6 The West Range and a section (right) of the North Range

7 The 'Drawing Room' in the North Range

IN·COMMEMORATION·OF·THE·DEFENCE·OF·THE·HONOURS·OF·SCOTLAND
FROM·SEPTEMBER·1651·TO·MAY·1652
BY·GEORGE·OGILVY·OF·BARRAS·GOVERNOR·OF·DUNNOTTAR·
AND·OF·THE·HELP·GIVEN·BY·HIS·WIFE·ELIZABETH·DOUGLAS
AND·BY·HER·KINSWOMAN·ANNE·LINDSAY

8 Close-up of the inscription above the drawing-room fireplace

9 The reservoir (outside the North Range)

10 The Silver House and the Chapel

Left: 11 The Chapel entrance

Below: 12 The Keep and the tunnel leading to the gateway

Right: 13 The entrance to the tunnel

Below: 14 The path leading from the castle to the roadway on the high ground

Opposite above: 15 Kinneff Old Church entrance (the sea-like area on the right is a field of barley)

Opposite below: 16 Kinneff Old Church

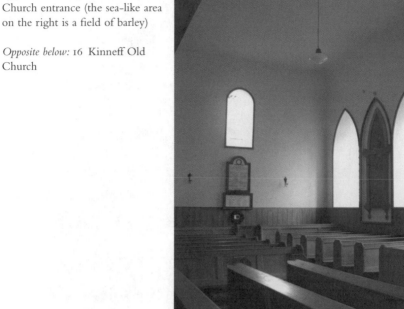

Right: 17 Church interior

Below: 18 Floral representation of the Regalia in the Old Church

19 The Ogilvie Memorial in the Old Church

20 The Grainger Memorial in the Old Church

21 The Kinneff Old Church Manse

7. That I did accordingly perform the same assurance in redelivering them to him:

This is the most notable untruth for they continued constantly in my custody until the day that, (according to his Majesty's command), I delivered them to the Earl Marschall in Dunnottar before many famous witnesses, of which my Lord Arbuthnott and the before written Sheriff Depute were two, I having kept them entire the space of nine years. Only a few days before the said delivery, Barrass, by a lying policy, to anticipate the Council's order, got the sceptre from me, upon his solemn oath to restore it upon my first desire. But this oath he broke, retaining the sceptre after I had earnestly required it. But this he did of purpose that he might pretend a hand in the delivery of the honours, on which pretence, he purchased a receipt on the whole honours from the Earl Marschall, upon which receipt, he grounded his lying petition, although the Earl Marschall's letter and another from Barrass to me, written the day before the honours were delivered, will testify that none but I either had them or delivered them.

10 – CHARLES II TO THE EARL OF MIDDLETON, 1662.

This letter is fairly self-explanatory although there could conceivably be some reason for the 'differences' between the Countess and her eldest son, the Earl Marschall, other than the 'ugly and unhandsome-carried business.'

May 8th, 1662.

Middleton, you are not, I am sure, a stranger to the great services were done in Scotland by my Lady Marschall at a time when few or none almost durst or would own me, therefore I need not tell you how just a sense I have of them and how desirous I am of any occasion to encourage her. Being lately informed that some differences have arisen betwixt her and her son in law [sic], the Earl Of Marschall (if any such shall happen),

I do particularly command you to see that no wrong be done her, but that she may enjoy what justly she has a pretension to, being a person that is very much in the care of your very affectionate friend, – Charles R.

II – TRANSCRIPT OF REGISTRY ENTRY RE: CHRISTIAN FLETCHER'S MARRIAGE TO LORD ABERCROMBIE 18 OCTOBER 1663.

This is the most that can be gleaned from the page recording the business of the Kinneff Kirk relative to Christian Fletcher's marriage to Lord Abercrombie. The right-hand side of the page is completely gone so it is impossible to provide a full transcript. Each line is missing an indeterminable number of words. Square brackets indicate characters that were either absent (due, e.g., to abbreviation) or illegible in the original document but capable of reconstruction either from the original abbreviation or from context. Pointed brackets enclose characters absent in the original document, due to damage to the paper, and either deduced from context or reconstructed from inference.

[4 October].

This day Collect[io]n gathered 13 s[hillings].

This day delated my Lord Abercrumie and …
sin of fornication ordained to be Sum[m]oned fo<r> …

11 October.

This day compeere[d] my Lord Abecrumie[;] tried [?] cons <erning> …
with Margaret Read, And the Said Lord being …
with Christian Fletcher in ordour to marey …
fitt to referr the bussines to the presbyte<ry> …
with both in reference to his satisfaction & in ref<erence> …

The sam day Margaret Read appoynted to be …
Collect[io]n 9 s[hillings]

18 October.

This day the minister did declair the judgme<nt> …
ordour to my Lord Abercrumie his bussines, for his …
ther was an act of the generall assemblie c[on]cern<ing> …
wer priviledged from the com[m]on p[en]a[n]ce [?] of repentance …
humble themselfes before the congregat[io]n in ther …
be satisfied[.] And as for his mareyage with …
advysed yt he shuld have no benefitt of the <illeg.> … <pro->
duce the extract of his divorce from his forme<r> …
gett it under the com[m]issares hand that such a …
Edinburgh[.]

This sam day the minister according to the …
did receave my Lord Abercrumie[.]

This day my Lord Abercrumie did produce …
Falconer his hand subscribed by true wittnesses th<at> …
was passed so that upon the product[io]n thereof …
c[on]tracted and proclaimed which was accordingli<e> …

Collect[io]n 13 s[hillings] 4 [pence] wherof iv s[hillings] is give<n> …

Also given to Andrew Moncurr 6 s[hillings] for go<ing> …
Read in the parich of Fetteresso[.]

[T]his [d]ay delated George John Simson[,] Jevrye Ble<?> …
f[or]m[er]ly James Moncurr for buying and …
day appoynted to c[om]peer against …

12 – ALEXANDER NISBET TO WILLIAM OGILVY.

By 1699, the war between Kintore and the Ogilvies seemed to have died a natural death until the narratives sent in for Alexander Nisbet's forthcoming book on heraldry once again put the cat among the pigeons.

> Sir, – I have received from your son several copies of evidents and instructions of your father's honourable trust and special fidelity in keeping and preserving the Honours of our nation in the worst of times, which are such convincing proofs of your father and mother's loyalty and honesty to their king and country that they well deserve to be published by an abler pen then mine. Yet Sir I shall not be wanting (since you have been pleased to communicate them to me) to perpetuate them in my designed treatise the best that I can to the deserved honour of your family. I doubt not of the verity of the copies, and your letter is convincing to me, yet it will be necessary that I see in your son's hands, or any other of your trustees, the principals again June next, that I may with greater assurance assert them to the world, Sir, your friend & humble servant, – Alexr. Nisbet

13 – A HISTORY OF THE EARL OF KINTORE.

The following is believed to be similar if not identical to the History of the Earldom of Kintore submitted to Nisbet in 1699 for inclusion in his *System of Heraldry*.

> A History of the first Earl of Kintore.

> John Keith, the seventh and youngest son to William Earl Marschall of Scotland, his mother being eldest daughter to John Earl of Mar sometime high treasurer of Scotland, was born at Leith upon the 13th day of February in the year of God one thousand six hundred and thirty three, who being scarcely three years of age when his father died, was virtuously educated by his mother both at schools and Marschall college in Aberdeen. I need

not say more as to his birth and quality being descended of the noble family of Marschall, of whose antiquity I refer the reader to the description of that ancient family. And now since it has pleased his Majesty, out of his Royal bounty, to confer, on the said John Keith, the title and dignity of the Earl of Kintore, it will not be amiss to discover some reason why the said John has arrived to the aforesaid honour.

After he was past schools, being just at the time when the present King Charles the second went out of Scotland with an army to England, where the Scots were unfortunately (by their overpowerful enemies, the English rebels) defeated at Worcester, he, being a youth, designed to go to France, and accordingly went away in February in the year of God 1652, for Holland, wherein his voyage at sea, was in great hazard of being cast away, there being many ships, the next day, whose wreck was discovered, but it pleased God that ship was preserved. Having arrived at Campheir in Zeland, he thought to have gone by sea to Calais, and so to Paris, but being twice beat by storm to Wlissen, resolved to go by land, which was very hazardous, by reason of the French and Spanish armies and garrisons that were so near others in Flanders. But at last having come to Lawbetton where a Scottish regiment was in garrison, he stayed there some little time and got three or four country gentlemen (by the favour of his countrymen) who paid contribution (as it's here called) to both French and Spaniard, to go alongst with him and in order to bring him to Arras.

But by the way near Dourleans, was attacked by a number of horsemen, and having taken him prisoner, they dismissed the country gentlemen without any damage done to them, and carrying him to a wood, where there was an old demolished chapel, made him come off his horse and presenting their carrabeans [carbines] to him (who had all that sort of arms) he, though he understood not their language yet did know well their design which was to kill him, did speak in Latin to them pleading pity for his life, which by the intercession of one of them, who seemed to have some command amongst them, and some compassion for him, and who only amongst them understood Latin, made them stop, and having spoke amongst themselves thereafter he told him that with much ado had he prevailed with the rest to spare his life, but that there was a necessity of taking all he had which immediately they did, stripping him of his clothes and taking all the gold and money he had upon him.

Whoever this man who under God saved him, did cause him ride behind another of that company, himself going along, and carried him to a peasant's house, and having got a little old coat with their country wooden shoes, ordered the country man to go alongst with him, back to Lawbetton, which after many miles going in that posture being in great hazard to be killed by the peasants if this man had not been with him, did happily come to these places where he was joyfully received by his countrymen who thought he had been killed, the country gentlemen who were formerly dismissed having come back and told them of his adventures.

Within few days thereafter, by the favour of that worthy gentleman, then Major Rutherford afterwards Earl of Teviot, got money from him, and there being a French gentleman who was going to Paris took the opportunity and went along with him, thereafter several hazards in their journey which were too tedious to relate, at last arrived in Paris at which time another misfortune attended him, for having money which he expected should have been answered him by bill, and as much as was destined to serve him for a whole year, his merchant broke, and so disappointing him of his money, rendered him near to a starving condition, were not that, by that famous gentleman (then Lieutenant General Middleton) thereafter Earl of Middleton his kindness, who brought him to a Scots factor, and upon his engagement gave him both money and clothes, then he carried him to the King who was then at the Louvre, his Majesty having made his escape out of England.

I give an account of this, the rather to show his misfortune in a time when all honest and loyal Scotsmen were never in a more sad and miserable condition, and particularly the Earl Marschall's family, the Earl his eldest brother with his second brother then Colonel George Keith now Earl Marschall being both prisoners at London, their whole estate was forfeited and in the English hands, they being only entertained by the kindness of their most virtuous mother, then Countess of Marschall, who had a considerable jointer, which (by the allseeing providence of God) she then enjoyed for her childrens' preservation.

In the meantime, the castle of Dunnottar, sometime before it was rendered to the English, the Honours of Scotland, the Crown, Sword and Sceptre, being there, the aforesaid Countess did go to the castle herself, and causing open the room where the Honours lay, ordered the then Governor, by name George Ogilvy, to cause remove them to some quiet and secure place (the castle in all appearance not being able to hold out long, by reason provision was like to fail, and all probability of supply stopped). Upon which, the Honours were conveyed out of Dunnottar very secretly to a very honest man Mr James Granger minister of Kinneff, and having buried them in that church, were there secured.

The castle being afterwards rendered up, the said George Ogilvy was dismissed unchallenged for the Honours only, upon bail, was obliged to appear on a call, but they having searched everywhere and missing them (their chief aim) did make prisoner George Ogilvy in Aberdeen and being severely put to it, for his only refuge did declare that, two or three months before, he had committed them to John Keith brother to the Earl Marschall (who was gone out of the kingdom) to be by him transported to the King, & for verifying thereof was forced to make up a receipt of them, by the said John which he owned & which being produced was the cause of the said George Ogilvy's preservation.

In the meantime this occasioned the said John Keith's banishment until an opportunity falling out of serving his Majesty, who laid commands upon Lieutenant General Middleton to go to Scotland by commission then made general of all the forces that had risen or were to rise there for restoration of his Majesty, and for recovery of his country's liberties. But the said John having fallen sick of an ague in Holland was not able to go immediately with the general yet, within a little time after having somewhat convalesced, did, with much difficulty, land in Scotland, and all the sea ports being secured, yet it pleased God, having put himself in disguise with a resolution to hazard himself in that service, did, with great diligence, get some horsemen with him, and having a correspondence with the late Marquis of Montrose did join with him, and met with the general at Dunkeld. And there after staying constantly with him till unhappily the English rebels coming on the Scots with overpowering numbers did defeat them at Lochgarioch, in the meantime he having come of with the general, who then retired to Lochaber with the few forces was left, and there being a necessity to separate, he going northward got occasion of a vessel and went abroad. And the said John with the Marquis of Montrose after many days wandering through the mountains with very few, the most part of their horse being left, were included in a capitulation with the English, all the rest having also capitulated.

In the meantime before he parted with General Middleton he showed him the more than ordinary hazard he was in lest he should fall in the English hands, after having owned the carrying abroad of the Honours he had nothing to instance the same, which might prove a means not only to ruin him but, likewise, put in hazard a discovery where the Honours were, upon which the general did grant a receipt of the Honours, as if by the Kings order he had received them at Paris, of the date June the eleventh in the year 1652 (his receipt is yet extant which I have seen and read) but in effect it was made up at Keppo in Lochaber in July 1654 which hereafter served to so good purpose that, having with my Lord Montrose capitulated with General Monk, was received by his order by Col Cobbet, then Governor of Dundee, who, when soon he saw him taken, he was ordered to enquire at him if he was the person of whom it was said, had carried away the Honours, who declared that it was he and upon production of General Middleton's receipt was believed that they were carried abroad, for which, as he was no more challenged, so was there no more noise of them nor search made after them till it pleased God, at his Majesty's happy restoration, the said John did go to London and having kissed the King, his Majesty was graciously pleased to look on him with kindness and conferred on him the office of Knight Marschall of Scotland, with a fee and salary annexed thereto of four hundred pounds sterling yearly, and the narrative of his patent being yet to be seen and which I thought fit here to insert bearing that:

'Having perfect knowledge of the work and loyalty of John Keith brother to the Earl Marschall whereof he was given good testimony at every occasion during the late troubles, and of the great service he performed in the entire preserving of his Majesty's Royal Honours, the Crown, Sword and Sceptre from the violence and possession of these rebels, that these years past have overrun and possessed themselves of his Majesty's Kingdom of Scotland, a service not to be forgotten by succeeding generations & which does justly entitle him to some honourable employment from his Majesty doth therefore by these presents constitute and create the said John Keith, Knight Marschall of the kingdom of Scotland etc.'

Yet notwithstanding of this favour, his reputation as being the true preserver of them, by the means above rehearsed, was like to be abused by the foresaid George Ogilvy who sent up his son to London and had the impudence to petition the King representing himself to be the only man that had preserved them, which as it is not to be denied but that he had a share in their safety by giving them out to the minister who also deserved a reward for his faithfulness in securing of them which the said John Keith ever acknowledged but it was an insufferable boldness for that George Ogilvy (whose father William Ogilvy being but in a mean employment as porter in Dunnottar) he may be thought to sute very ill with his son to attempt the lessening the honour and the truth of such an action of a son of that family where both his father and himself attained to there cheifest credit by being servants to it.

However the King did make the said George Ogilvy Knight Baronet and gave him a pension, a reward which sufficiently might have satisfied him and whereat the said John did never repine, and as for the minister who was a most honest man, and who still acknowledged the said John Keith to be the only means of preserving them as I have seen in a narration written and subscribed under the minister's own hand attributing to him the honour as the prime instrument of their safety, which by owning the transporting of them abroad did stop the enemy from searching for them and also freed the said George Ogilvy from prison and further trial the date of this declaration is the 19 of October 1660.

This honest minister was by order of Parliament holden by the Earl of Middleton, recommended to get some money out of the treasury but the honest man shortly dying thereafter got it not, and his relict and children being yet as I suppose alive, deserves certainly a reward, for the which end the said John would very willingly contribute his endeavours.

There was the necessity of being so tedious upon this account to vindicate the said John now Earl of Kintore of all lies and aspersions that might seemingly interrupt the honour he has acquired by being the instrument of their preservation. For which cause and for other services done by him his Majesty to his honour has graciously continued his favour for him, and having made him one of his Privy Council some years ago has since nobilitated him with the title and dignity of Earl of Kintore Lord Inverrurie & Keithhall etc. The narrative of his patent being about the same strain of that of the office of Knight Marschall above rehearsed, he is still alive and having married a daughter of the Earl of Haddington (whose mother was a daughter of George Marquess of Huntly) has four sons and two daughters.

As for his estate, his lands are all seated in the shire of Aberdeen having the greatest interest in the two little towns of Kintore and Inverurie which are two royal boroughs which are situated upon the river of Don and water of Urie, the rest of his lands being upon the said waters, his principal house being called Keithhall, lies upon the water of Urie the town of Inverurie being situated over against it, and the water running betwixt these two places not being much above a quarter of mile's distance from other, is reputed one of the pleasantest seats in all that shire, he has also several other houses and lands adjacent to them such as Ardeharrall in the parish of Mountkeigie, Fornat in the parish of Keithhall, Skene and Halforrest in the parish of Kintore this last being an old castle only, famous by being built by King Robert Bruce who, while he had war against the Cumins, had much residence there.

14 – THE ACHIEVEMENT OF GEORGE OGILVY OF BARRASS.

In the renewed dispute, in the early 1700s, between the Earl of Kintore and the family of Ogilvy of Barrass, the Earl's submission of his story to Nisbet was the *casus belli* but the first shot fired appears to be William Ogilvy's publication of this document, a pamphlet entitled 'The Achievement of George Ogilvy of Barrass, Knight and Baronet, sometime Governor of Dunnottar and Preserver of the Regalia.' This, like the subsequently published 'Vindication', is quite interesting since it comprises, nearly fifty years after the principal events, William Ogilvy's recollections and beliefs:

Argent a Lion Passant, Guardant, crowned with an Imperial Crown, holding in his dexter paw a Sword, gules, in Pale, Hilted and Pommelled Or, in the dexter chief point a Thistle Proper, ensigned with a Crown of the last, and in the sinister the Badge of Nova Scotia, as a Knight Barronet; which Shield is Timbered with Helmet and Cachements befitting his degree, on a Wreath of his Tinctures, for Crest a Demi-man armed at all points, pointing furth his right hand towards the Motto on an Escroll, Praeclarum Regi & Regno Servitium, Which Blazon is thus Matriculated 27th December 1673.

This family carries the Lyon passant, Guardant, for the paternal coat of Oglivie, The Sword, Crown and Thistle, as additional figures of honour granted to him by authority, for special and eminent service done to his King and country, in preserving the Honours of Scotland from falling into the hands of the English (intimated by his motto, Praeclarum Regi & Regno Servitium) as is evident from the following account instructed by principal papers and evidents. For 'tis more satisfactory to man to know the truth of things as they were really designed and acted from the testimony of original papers and documents, then from the allegations and bare assertions of pretenders, without proof or instruction.

When the rebels in Brittain under Oliver Cromwell the usurper, had triumphed over the best of men, and justest of kings, Charles the first, and those that persisted in their loyalty to him in these lamentable times of confusion, the Regalia or Honours of Scotland were delivered to the custody of the Earl Marschall, and were lodged in the strong Castle of Dunnottar, within the shire of Mearns, as a place of greatest security and distance from the enemy.

The said Earl being obliged to be in the fields to defend his King and country against the usurper, he made choice of George Ogilvy of Barrass, as the fittest man for his valour, prudence and loyalty, to entrust the keeping of the said Castle of Dunnottar with the Honours, viz. the Crown, Sceptre and Sword, and other monuments of the kingdom therein, makes him his lieutenant, and gives him the commission following:

'Forasmuch as the Kings Majesty and Committee of Estates, have entrusted the care and keeping of the house and castle of Dunnottar to us William Earl Marschall, and have allowed forty men, a lieutenant, and two sergeants to be entertained within it upon the public charge, therefore we do hereby nominate George Ogilvy of Barrass to be our lieutenant for keeping of the said house and castle, and gives unto him the sole and full power of the command thereof, and of the men that are to be entertained therein for keeping thereof under us, with power to him to bruick, enjoy, and keep the said place, with all fees, dues and allowances belonging thereto, as fully in all respects as any other lieutenant in such a case may do. In witness whereof, we have subscribed these presents at Stirling the Eighth day of July 1651. – Sic Subscribitur, Marschall.
Archibald Primrose Witness.
William Keith Witness.
Alexander Lindsay Witness.'

The Earl Marschall having entrusted as said is the government of the said castle, and the Honours therein to George Ogilvie, he accompanies the King to England, and after the battle of Worcester, was taken by the English and carried to London, where he was detained prisoner in the Tower for a long time.

George Ogilvy of Barrass being sole keeper of the Honours, and governor of the said castle, which he found not sufficiently provided with men, ammunition, and other provisions, to hold out against a long siege, as the King had ordered, acquaints John Campbell Earl of Loudon then Chancellor, who returned him the following answer.

'Sir, – Your Letter of the last of October, came to my hands the 9th of November instant, and the Parliament being appointed to meet here upon the 12 day, I stayed the bearer, in expectation that I might return you the Parliaments answer and orders, but the Parliament not having met, and there being no meeting of the Committee of Estates, I can give you no positive advice nor order, but I conceive that the trust committed to you, and the safe custody of these things under your charge, did require that provisions, a competent number of honest stout soldiers, and other necessaries should have been provided and put in the Castle, before you had been in any hazard.

And if you be in a good condition, or that you can supply your self with all necessaries, and that the place be tenable against all attempts of the enemy, I doubt not but you will hold out, but if you want provisions, soldiers and ammunition, and cannot hold out against all the assaults of the enemy, which is feared you cannot do, if hard put to it, I know no better expedient than that the Honours be speedily and safely transported to some remote and strong castle in the Highlands.

And I wish you had delivered them to the Lord Balcarras, as was desired by the Committee of Estates, nor do I know any better way for the preservation of these things and your exoneration. And it will be an irreparable loss and shame, if these things shall be taken by the enemy, and very dishonourable for your self. I have here retained your letter to the Lord Balcarras, hearing he is still in the North, and not come to this country. I have written to Sir John Smith, to furnish you the remainder of the victuals you wrote he should have given you; If he be in the North you will send it is him, and if he be gone home to Edinburgh, I cannot help it. So having given you the best advice I can at present, I trust you will with all care and faithfulness be answerable according to the trust committed to you, and I shall continue your assured and real friend, − Sic Subscribitur, Loudon Cancelr

Dated at Finlarge 13th November.

Direct thus, For my much Respected Friend George Ogilvy Governor of Dunnottar.'

The Governor George Ogilvy being disappointed of sufficient force and provisions, to hold out a long siege, and observing the advances the English made daily in reducing the nation, was exceedingly perplexed, how to prevent the enemies getting the Honours of this kingdom in their hands. He advises with his wife, (a lady of great prudence and undaunted courage.) She therefore forms a very happy contrivance, that she should convey the Honours privately out of the castle, and secure them without her husbands knowledge, that when he should be put to it, and tortured by the enemy, he might freely declare he knew not where they were. In order thereto, this lady sends for Mr James Granger minister of Kinneff his wife, in whom she had great confidence, and imparts to her the design, she promising to be faithful. They privately carried the Honours out of the said castle to Mr James Granger the minister, (the other trustee,) and put them under ground within the church of Kinneff. And the manner how the Honours were transported from the castle thither, was on a servant-woman's back, in a sack amongst hards of lint.

George Ogilvy the governor, not being able to hold out the castle against so powerful an enemy, that then besieged him so close, and expecting no relief, and all other forts and castles in the kingdom being in the enemies possession, enters into capitulation with Colonel Thomas Morgan, and surrenders on honourable terms, the garrison being permitted to march out of the said castle with drums beating, and colours flying, which were carried by the present Sir William Ogilvy of Barrass son to the said Capt. George, (who was the last person who carried colours at that time in Scotland for the King). And one of the articles of capitulation being to deliver up the Honours, (for the English were certainly informed they were in the castle) or give a rational account of them. These are the very words of capitulation, which the present Sir William, (the said Captain George his son) hath in his custody.

After the surrender, the English demanded the Honours, or an account of them. The governor declared he knew not where they were, for his wife had privately taken them away, without acquainting him. upon which he was put into close prison in the said castle. His lady being examined and threatened with torture, she boldly affirmed by way of evasion for her own safety, that she had delivered the Honours to John Keith, (now Earl of Kintore) who carried them abroad to the King. But the English distrusting her, put her in close prison also, and sent out a party to the house of Barrass, to apprehend the said Sir William Ogilvie, (their only son and child) that they might torture him in sight of his parents, to extort a confession from them, but he by providence made a timely escape, and underwent much toil and fatigue, by travelling night and day, till he came to his friends in Angus where he remained incognito.

After the said Capt. George and his lady had been close prisoners for a year, in which time they suffered much inhumane usage, by the cruelty of the English, who caused a sentinel stand at the prison door, and another at the prisoners bedside, that they should not commune about the Honours. And after all, the said Capt. George and his lady adhering to their former declarations, that the Honours were carried abroad by the now Earl of Kintore, had such an appearance of truth, that upon mediation of friends, Major-General Dean was prevailed upon to grant them liberty to go to their own house of Barrass, upon such conditions as here follows, conform to the principal warrant.

'Whereas in the capitulation made upon the surrender of the Castle of Dunnottar, between Colonel Thomas Morgan and Captain George Ogilvy the then Governor, it was among other things agreed that the said Captain George Ogilvy should deliver up the Crown, Sword, and Sceptre of the late King of Scots, which were in his custody, or give a good account thereof. And forasmuch as, I have caused the said Captain Ogilvy ever since that time to be retained a prisoner in the said castle, for not delivering the said Crown, Sword, and Sceptre, or giving a good account thereof. Now in regard he makes diverse pretences that the said Crown, Sword and Sceptre were taken away out of Dunnottar without his knowledge. And lastly his wife conveyed the same to a gentleman that carried them to foreign parts. I am willing that in case he shall procure good security of 2000 or 1500 Lib. Sterl. that he shall render himself a true prisoner to you upon demand; As also that his wife shall do the like, he shall have his liberty out of the castle unto his own house, being seated within four miles of the same, providing he do not at all go from the house above three miles. And I do hereby authorize you to receive such bond of him as said is, for his and his wife's forthcoming, and thereupon to give him the liberty abovementioned, for which this shall be your warrant, dated the third of December 1652. Sic Subscribitur, – Ri: Dean. Direct to Captain Garnor, the present Governor of Dunnottar.'

Upon this warrant Captain George and his Lady were set at liberty, and Robert Grahame of Morphie became cautioner for them, as by the following bond:

'Whereas the Right Honourable Major General Richard Dean, hath issued an order unto Captain John Garnor now Governor of Dunnottar, that he grants liberty to Captain George Ogilvie, together with his wife (they being both prisoners in the said garrison) to repair to their dwelling house, providing they give sufficient security, that they depart not above three miles from Barrass, being their habitation, and that they or either of them act nothing that is or may be prejudicial to the Parliament of the Commonwealth of England; And likewise on advertisement or warning given, they present themselves true prisoners at Dunnottar Castle, to the governor thereof or his depute, and that the said Capt. Ogilvy and his wife shall perform the abovesaid Articles. I whose name is underwritten, do bind my self, my heirs, executors, and administrators, under the penalty and forfaulture of 2000 Lib. of lawful current English money, in case of failing to present, enter again, and make forthcoming the said prisoners, when the governor shall send for them. In witness whereof, I have hereunto put my hand and seal, the 10th of January 1653. Sic subscribitur, Robert Grahame of Morphie.
Attested by: Richard Hughes, John Turner.'

Sometime after this, the said Captain George and his lady were necessitat and enforced by the rigidity and strictness of the English, to find security of new, as the following bond doth evince.

'Whereas upon solicitation for Capt. George Ogilvy and his wife's further enlargement, the Honourable Colonel Lilburn Commander in Chief of all the forces in Scotland, hath ordered Captain Garnor of Dunnottar Castle upon security given, to give them six weeks time to go about their lawful affairs. I do therefore engage my self my heirs, executors, administrators, assignees in the sum of five hundred pounds of good and lawful English money, for their personal appearance into the former obligation of confinement, six weeks after the date hereof; In witness hereof, I have put my hand and seal, the 1st of February 1653. Sic subscribitur, James Anderson.

Attested by John Barkley, Richard Hughes.'

Under this restraint Captain Ogilvies lady dyed, and he remain'd therein till the restoration of King Charles the 2nd and all that time had a special care of the Honours, by sending monthly clean linen to Mr James Granger the minister, and his wife, with instructions to take them out of the ground, and wrap them in the same least they should be spoiled or tarnished, which the minister of Kinneff and his wife punctually observed, and were faithful in their secrecy, till the King's restoration, (for which they had a pecunial reward), and then delivered them to the said Capt. George, who according to the King's order, did redeliver them to the Earl Marschall in as good condition as he at first received them, as is evident by the following receipt, which will demonstratively and undeniably prove, that the foresaid Capt. George and his lady were the principal keepers and preservers of the Honours of Scotland, (whatever others pretend) and the only sufferers therefore. Which honourable piece of service, so faithfully performed, should never be forgot by King or country, in saving of the Honours, which prevented both the disgrace of the kingdom, and the irreparable loss of our ancient regalia.

But notwithstanding of this noble and good service done by the said Capt. George and his lady, yet at King Charles the 2nd his restoration. the then old Countess Marschall wrote to His Majesty, that her son John Keith, now Earl of Kintore, (who was then abroad upon his travels, and knew nothing of the matter) had preserved the Honours, being that the said Capt. George had unwarily imparted to the said Countess where they were hid, and how by that contrivance of his wife in affirming that she had delivered them to the said John Keith, they had saved themselves and concealed the Honours from the English. And His Majesty knowing nothing of Captain George Ogilvy and his lady's special service in preserving of the Honours (in respect they did not timely apply) did upon the said Countess her misrepresentation, create her said son, first Knight Marschall of Scotland, and then Earl of Kintore, and ordered him a pension of 400 Lib. Sterl. a year, which he enjoyed all King Charles the 2nd his lifetime, and is as yet continued to him with the said place and dignity, for his pretended preservation of the Honours.

Captain George Ogilvie, then in the mean time in Scotland, being informed that the foresaid Countess and others had misrepresented to his Majesty his faithful service, in preserving of the Honours, by which he was like to lose the honour and merit of so noble and eminent an action, performed with the hazard of his own and his lady's life, with the ruin of his fortune. He sends to London his son, the said Sir William Ogilvy of Barrass, to give a true relation of the preservation of the Honours, who addresses his Majesty with the following petition.

'To the King's most Excellent Majesty.
The Humble Petition of William Ogilvie, Son to George Ogilvy of Barrass, Sheweth,
that whereas your petitioner is sent up here by his father, to give your Majesty notice that his said father hath had, and still preserves the Crown, Sceptre and Sword of Scotland in his custody, long before the English possessed the castle of Dunnottar, with the great hazard of his Life, and long and strait imprisonment, which occasioned the death of his wife. And in respect of your petitioners father his great interest with these honours, he could not desert that great charge, to come here and attend your Majesty himself. Wherefore he hath sent your petitioner to have your Majesty's particular order, in relation to the foresaids Honours.'

The Answer to the Petition was as follows:

'Whitehall, 28 September 1660
His Majesty ordains the petitioners father to deliver his Crown, Sceptre and Sword, to the Earl Marschall of Scotland, and to get his receipt of them. – Sic subscribitur, Lauderdale.'

This order was by the then Earl of Lauderdale's advice, who said if John Keith had kept the Honours, then the said George Ogilvy was not able to deliver them, But if the said George had the keeping of them, 'twould evidently and undeniably appear who was the true preserver.

At this time the then old Countess Marschall being informed that the Honours were hid in the church of Kinneff, she endeavours by all means to persuade Mr James Granger, the minister, to deliver them to her, but Capt. George getting a surmise thereof, goes to the said church, and takes out the Sceptre, and carries it to his House of Barrass, and takes also an obligement from the said minister to make the rest of the Honours forthcoming to him, as appears by his obligement, whereof the tenor follows.

'Whereas I have received a discharge from George Ogilvy of Barrass of the Honours of this kingdom, and he hath got no more but the sceptre, therefore I oblige myself, that the rest, viz.: The Crown and Sword, shall be forthcoming at demand, by this my ticket, written and subscribed this same day I received the discharge, 28th September 1660. – Sic Subscribitur, Mr J. Granger.'

Within few days thereafter, Capt. George gets the King's order to deliver up to the Earl Marschall the Crown, Sceptre, and Sword, which readily he obeys, and gets the Earls following receipt, all written with his own hand.

'At Dunnottar the 8th day of October 1660, I William Earl Marschall, grants me to have received from George Ogilvy of Barrass, the Crown, Sword and Sceptre, the ancient monuments of this kingdom, entire and complete, in the same condition they were entrusted by me to him and discharges the foresaid George Ogilvy of his receipt thereof, by this my subscription, day and place foresaid, – Sic subscribitur, Marschall.'

Capt. George Ogilvy not only preserved by his prudence, fidelity and diligent care, the Honours as said is, but also considerable writs and monuments entrusted to him when governor of Dunnottar, (the way and manner too tedious to insert,) such as the King's papers, the receipt whereof follows.

'We William Earl Marschall grant us to have received from George Ogilvie, sometime governor of our castle of Dunnottar, some papers belonging to the King's Majesty, which were in Dunnottar the time of his being Governor there, in two little coffers, which papers consisting to the number of eight score sixteen several pieces, whereof there are four packets sealed, and one broke open, of which papers I grant the receipt, and obliges me to warrant the said George at His Majesty's hands, and all others whatsoever, by this my warrant, signed, sealed, and subscribed at London, the first of December 1655. – Sic Subscribitur, Marschall.'

The said Capt. George also preserved the registers and papers of the Kirk of Scotland which is evident by a receipt thereof, granted to him by the Lord Balcarras, by order of a commission from the Kirk. Also the monuments and charters of the University of St Andrews, which he delivered to Robert Yuill, upon the order of Robert Honnyman, Clerk to the University, and got his receipt thereof. And suchlike, the principal papers and charters belonging to the family of Hamilton which he delivered to James Hamilton, then servant to the present Duchess Dowager of Hamilton, and got his receipt thereof, written on the end of my Lady Duchess her letter, brought by him to the said Capt. George. All which principal receipts and documents are registered (for preservation) in the Books of Council and Session, being the General Register of this Kingdom.

Captain George Ogilvy having faithfully exonerated himself of the foresaids trusts, takes journey for London, to wait upon the King, by whom he was kindly received, and delivered to his Majesty the Earl Marschall's receipt of the Honours, which the King having read, Captain George humbly requested it back, that it might be kept in his family as an evident of his and his wife's loyalty and good service done to the King and kingdom of Scotland, which his Majesty granted, and was graciously pleased to confer a deserved mark of his Highness favour upon him and his family, by making him a Knight Baronet, by a patent dated at Whitehall 5th March 1661, and gave him a new charter of the lands of Barrass, changing the holding thereof, to hold thereafter blench of his Majesty and his Successors, 3rd March 1662, which is ratified in Parliament 11th August 1679. In which patent, charter and ratification, is narrated the eminent service done and performed by Sir George Ogilvy of Barrass, and that he was the preserver of his Majesty's Crown, Sword and Sceptre, the ancient Honours of the Kingdom of Scotland, and the damages sustained by the said Sir George and his lady there through, from the beginning of the usurpation, during which time (notwithstanding of all temptations and threatening used against them by the usurper) they carried themselves with the greatest integrity and constancy under all their sufferings.

This Sir George Ogilvy of Barrass was descended of the honourable family of Ogilvy Earl of Airlie. He Married Elizabeth Douglas, daughter of Mr John Douglas of Barrass, brother german to William Earl of Angus, grand-father to the late Duke of Hamilton. By this Lady he had the present Sir William Ogilvie, who married Isabel Ogilvy daughter to Sir John Ogilvy of Inverearity, by whom he hath very hopeful children.

15 – A VINDICATION FOR PUBLISHING THE 'ACHIEVEMENT'.

The following 'Vindication' makes the fairly reasonable (but hopeless) case that Ogilvy's 'Account' was produced not to defame the Earl of Kintore but to defend the good name of George Ogilvy and of his wife, Elizabeth Douglas:

A Clear Vindication and Just Defence For Publishing of the Foregoing account. With other Remarkable Instances, and Observable Passages, relating to, and Confirming the Truth of it.

For Truth seeks no Corners, fears no Discovery, and Justice is no Respecter of Persons.

That the publishing an account of the preservation of Crown, Sword, and Sceptre of Scotland, from falling into the hands of the English usurpers, by Sir George Ogilvy of Barrass (then governor of Dunnottar Castle) and Dame Elizabeth Douglas his lady, was not done of design to offend, or derogate from the just honour of any, far less those of the family of Marschall (for whom the said Sir George Ogilvy did on all occasions evidence, and his posterity do yet continue a grand veneration and due regard.) But there being an account of the Earl of Kintore's family given to be insert in Mr Alexander Nisbet his book of heraldry, in which account, the sole and chief preservation of the Honours is ascribed to the now Earl of Kintore, and the then Countess Dowager Marschall his mother, and not only makes mention of the said Sir George in a dishonourable manner, but doth also smother (and might in process of time have totally obliterate) the good service, loyalty, and sufferings of the said Sir George his well-deserving lady. And it being credibly reported, that at the same juncture the said Earl's account was given to Mr Nisbet at Edinburgh, the like account was sent to London, to be insert in Morerey's Dictionary (and that a long time before the printing and publishing of Sir George's Account).

What less could have been done than, in self defence, to vindicate the fame and good name, and to perpetuate the sufferings of the said Sir George, and his lady. For the consideration, that the good name and reputation of the righteous shall be vindicated and secured after death is, to a generous nature, sensible of true honour, a great spur and encouragement to worthy and virtuous deeds, and the earnest desire that people of old had of leaving a good name behind them, and of perpetuating the fame and glory of their actions to after ages did animate their brave spirits in the pursuit of virtue and, with the hazard of their lives, to do great and glorious exploits for their country. And as it is the argument of a great mind to be moved by this consideration, so it's a sign of a low and base spirit to neglect it.

Besides, there's a certain civility in human nature, which will not suffer men to wrong the dead, and to deny them the just commendation of their worth.

I say what less could have been done, than to vindicate the good name and reputation, and to perpetuate the sufferings of the deceast Sir George

Ogilvy and his lady by publishing to the world the true matter of fact in the whole contrivance and procedure, from the evident instructions and documents left by the said Sir George, and the account of the transactions, and pregnant circumstances clearly by him narrated, which it's presumed will abundantly satisfy all unprejudiced and unbiased persons, that the said Sir George and his lady were the only sufferers for, and preservers of the Honours. But particularly his lady, being of an heroic and masculine spirit, like the brave old Douglas, was eminently and mainly instrumental (by the divine aid) in preserving of the Honours, as anon will more fully appear.

For Sir George's lady not only conveyed the Honours out of the said castle, by her special care and contrivance, without her husband's privity and knowledge, but gave out and maintained, both for concealing of the Honours in a feasible way, and as a means of her own and her husband's safety, and exemption from torture, that she had delivered the Honours to the now Earl of Kintore, who had carried them abroad to the King and to confirm the English that 'twas so, Sir George's Lady (being of a ready and accurate wit) contrived a missive letter, as if from the now Earl of Kintore, giving her an account, that the Crown, Sword and Sceptre of Scotland, were safely delivered by him to the King, which letter the English intercepting, she having so ordered the matter that it should fall into their hands, did thereafter almost believe it to be true, but before that was done, the English menaced and vial-treated Sir George (and his lady in particular) to the highest degree of cruelty, in so far as Colonel Morgan was upon the point to expose her to an exquisite torment, by putting her in the boots, and he said, she was the most resolute and undaunted woman ere he spoke to, for she bid him do his utmost, she'd give him no further account of the Honours.

And that the English were intending to have wreaked their fury on Sir George and his lady, may be shrewdly guessed, by their causing a sentinel stand at the prison door, and another at the prisoners bedside all night, that they (Sir George and his lady) should not commune nor converse anent the securing and concealing of the Honours and because Sir George's lady bravely and constantly maintained, that she had delivered the Honours to the now Earl of Kintore, as aforesaid, they to disgrace and affront her the more, caused their provost-martial to attend her, when she obtained the liberty and favour to take the air for some hours within the precinct of the castle, she being then almost stifled by a close and squalid imprisonment, which certainly hastened, if not procured her death, being a woman of a high and fine spirit, that would rather (like a piece of true steel) break than yield.

For, in a little time after Sir Robert Grahame of Morphie's becoming bail for her and her said husband's rendering themselves prisoners again to the English governor of Dunnottar Castle upon demand, she became hectic, being then almost worn-out, both by her former long and strait imprisonment, and by the deep impressions the immoderate care of preserving the Honours had made on her, to which being added, the thoughts of her remaining still under restraint, and the continual damps of re-entering to close prison. No wonder that her high and noble spirit, being as unconquerable as she had then made the Honours, broke the prison of her body by a happy and peaceable death, to enjoy, as there's good reason to hope, a crown of glory, being the promised reward of the righteous.

And as this lady excelled in piety and virtue, so there's one very remarkable instance of her steady integrity, (which should eternize her name): that when she was on her deathbed, she then, and not till then, did impart to Sir George her husband, how, and where the honours were hid and reposited, and took his hand upon oath, that although he should be brought to the scaffold to be execute, he should never betray his trust, nor deliver up the honours to the English.

So by what is above narrated, 'twill unquestionably appear, that neither the now Earl of Kintore, nor his mother, were either privy to, or had a hand in conveying the honours out of the said castle, nor in securing and hiding of them. But after the thing was providentially and happily done, for Sir George's lady to make use of the now Earl of Kintore his name, was a very lawful stratagem in her, and that which no generous man then abroad would have declined to own, but would not have reaped the fruits of Sir George and his lady's labours, nor taken the whole reward due for their sufferings. And that lady might have made use of his name (if Providence had suggested it), who was wont to come from King Charles the second, then in exile, to get account of the posture the castle and garrison of Dunnottar was in, and likewise to know how matters then stood in this kingdom. And for instance that Sir John Strachan did so, he brought a letter writ with King Charles's own hand, under cover of one from the then Lieutenant General Middleton, directed thus, to the governor and gentlemen in the castle of Dunnottar, which letters are yet extant, packed up, and folded in the most secret and compendious manner. The tenor of the King's letter is verbatim as follows.

'Gentlemen, assure your selves I am very careful of you, and sensible of your affection to me. Give credit to what this bearer shall say to you, and observe any directions you shall receive from Lieutenant General Middleton. you shall shortly hear again from me, and I would have you find some way frequently to advertise me of your condition, which I will take all possible care to relieve.

Paris, March 26th. 1652. – Charles R.'

The tenor of Middleton's letter to the governor is verbatim as follows:

'My dear friend, I am so overjoyed to hear, that you in this time do behave yourself so gallantly, that I shall be most desirous to do you service, the particulars I remit to the bearer my cousin and yours, to whom give trust, since he is particularly instructed from him who shall rather perish, than be wanting to his friend, and who, in all conditions, is, and shall be, yours, – J.M.'

The bearer, as is said before, was Sir John Strachan.

By these letters it doth further appear, that Sir George Ogilvy (then governor of Dunnottar Castle) could not have carried himself with more loyalty and gallantry than he did, and although it be acknowledged in one part of the now Earl of Kintore's account, given to Mr Nisbet, that there could be (then) no hopes of succour, nor the said castle able to hold out long, if once attacked, yet, in an other part of the Earl's account, it's alleged, that after Colonel Morgan had laid siege to Dunnottar Castle, and that the cannon had played against it two days, the governor capitulated for himself alone, and made the English masters of the place, by which they got all the furniture, plate, pictures, books, and ancient papers belonging to the family of Marschall.

To which it's answered, that there being no relief given, and all hopes thereof being then cut off, and but thirty six men in the garrison, (a mere handful in comparison of the number then requisite to defend the place) and all of them day and night upon duty, were extremely fatigued and over-waked, yet they maintained their respective posts valorously for the space of ten days, during which time the said castle was bombarded, and also battered by the cannon of the English. And when the governor found, that the garrison was not able to hold out longer, and all other forts within the kingdom being then reduced, and under command of the English, and the main chance being secured, and preserved by his lady, viz. the honours, and the King's papers, the said Sir George (the governor) made an honourable capitulation, the garrison being permitted to march out of the said castle with colours flying, drums beating, and kindled matches, for the space of a mile from the place. And the English were astonished to admiration, to see such a small force make so long and vigorous resistance against such a prevailing army. And the English expressly told, that if the castle had not been that day surrendered, they were resolved to have stormed it the very next day following, which easily they might have done, considering (as aforesaid) the bad posture the garrison was in.

And that which did (sometime before) mightily incommode and perplex Sir George the governor, was a mutiny raised and fomented by one David Lighton, who had been a colonel abroad, yet by the said governor's prudence, diligence and conduct, the mutiny was suppressed and crushed in the bud, by causing train-out Colonel Lighton, and never allowed him to re-enter the castle, whereby the soldiers were quashed and composed, and the direful effects of that mutiny prevented, which was to have sacrificed the governor, and all under his charge, to the merciless cruelty of the English. And 'twas a signal act of Providence the design was discovered, for there being several veteran soldiers in the garrison, who had served in France and other places, most of them strangers to the governor, and getting no pay from the public, made the governor's post uneasy, and also brought him to a deal of charges, he being necessitat to give pay to the said Colonel Lighton, and also, to the surgeon, engineer and cannoneer, all out of his own pocket, he having got no pay either to himself or them, from the public.

The manner how the King's papers were conveyed out of the castle was thus, the governor's lady made a girdle of linen, and packed them up, and sowed them in so dextrously, that no part of the girdle appeared more bulkish than t'other, and they were happily carried out about a young gentlewoman's middle, whom the said governor's lady had kept in the said castle as a friend (for a while before) on that design.

And after the castle was surrendered, as aforesaid, and that Sir George (the governor) and his lady were cast in prison by the English, their own private estate was not only mismanaged and neglected, but the generality of the country and neighbourhood looked upon Sir George and his lady as forlorn persons, and upon their fortune as ruined, in so much that those to whom they were indebted did instantly distress them. And the English did harass them by seizing upon and away taking of the horses which laboured their own Mains of Barrass, and Sir George and his lady were not only enforced to suffer all this, but were also necessitate to be at great charges, during the time of their imprisonment, in complementing and treating the officers and soldiers of the English garrison, out of their private estate, and the doing whereof was the great means (under the divine protection) of Sir George and his lady's preservation from the extreme cruelty and torture they were threatened with by the English.

And after Sir George his lady had, by her resolution and constancy, baffled all the threats and bad usage of the English, they (the English) proffered her and her said husband a vast sum of money for the Honours, but that bait, though very prevalent with a great part of mankind, did not in the least stagger Sir George nor his lady's resolutions of integrity and loyalty, which was as firm, as the rock on which they were then imprisoned, and remained untainted to the end, et finis coronat opus. So that bribes were not able to allure them, nor threats to frighten them into a discovery of these notable Regalia, the ancient monuments of this kingdom.

And the said Sir George was so cautious and circumspect as to keep and leave to his posterity, as an evidence of his and his lady's loyalty, not only all the most material papers relative to the preservation of the Honours, but also, all the missive letters sent him thereabout, with the doubles of his own returns and answers, and all the passes granted by the English to him and his lady (from time to time) during their restraint and confinement to the house of Barrass. And the said Sir George did also leave to posterity memoirs of the most remarkable instances, and observable passages that occurred and fell out anent his and his lady's sufferings and losses in preserving of the honours, without which adminicles, 'twas not possible to have writ truly on this subject. But there's as much sure evidence, fairly exhibited, for proving the truth of what's asserted, as can be reasonably expected, or the nature of the thing can bear, or require, and doth so irrefragably convince all, as to leave them nothing to say against it, unless there be any who will obstinately say, we will not believe it, nor yet our own eyes, nor the verdict of our reason.

And that the now Earl of Kintore and his mother did ascribe to themselves the chief and sole preservation of the honours, and did so inform King Charles II at his restoration (before Sir George Ogilvy was able to apply, having then the Honours under his care), is evident both by the narrative of the said Earl's account given to Mr Nisbet, and also by the answer given by King Charles to the then Earl of Strafford, when the late Earl of Airly (then Lord Ogilvy) did solicit Strafford to represent to his Majesty the eminent service done by the said Sir George Ogilvy and his lady in preserving the honours of Scotland. 'By my Lord Ogilvy's good leave,' said the king, 'it must not be so, for my Lady Marschall wrote to me, that she and her son John had preserved the honours.' This the late Airlie did aver to be the King's answer.

And that the said Countess endeavoured to procure Mr James Granger, then minister of Kinneff, to deliver up the Honours to her, is evident by her sending of Robert Keith of Whiteriggs (then Sheriff Depute of the Mearns) to persuade him thereto, but Sir George getting a surmise of the design, did expostulate with the said minister thereabout, who the more to ascertain the said Sir George, wrote him a letter, wherein he expressly says, 'I'll break my neck before I break to you.' These are Mr Granger's own words, yet Sir George to prevent such endeavours, went and took up the sceptre to his house of Barrass, and at the same time got an obligement from the minister, to make the crown and sword forthcoming to him upon demand. And Sir George after he had taken up the sceptre, said to the minister, 'the piper plays the worse that wants the nether shafts,' (being an old Scottish maxim) intimating thereby, that the said Countess her design was rendered abortive.

And although the said minister's wife got a pecunial reward for her and her husband's fidelity and secrecy, (who were employed by Sir George's lady as trustees for hiding of the honours) yet notwithstanding of all the good and loyal service so well contrived, prudently managed, and faithfully performed by Sir George and his Lady, (who were under God the prime actors, the only sufferers for, and main preservers of the Honours) neither he the said Sir George, nor his son Sir William got either place, pension, or any pecunial reward. But when Sir George, after the King's restoration, and that he had delivered the honours to the Earl Marschall, and got the Earl's receipt of them, went to London, and was kindly received by the King, and was made a Knight Baronet, and got the change of the holding of his lands, and the promise of a pension, how soon the King's revenues were settled.

And sometime thereafter, the present Sir William went up to court (a second time) in expectation of the pension promised his father Sir George. And although King Charles the 2nd was graciously pleased to say, from his own mouth, to the present Sir William, (upon his reminding the King of Sir George and his lady's losses and sufferings in preserving of the Honours), 'be you confident, I'll see to the standing of your family.' Yet the then Lauderdale, who was sole secretary, postponed and wearied out the said Sir William with dilators and shifts, to the great loss of his money and time at court. And after Sir William had long waited, he was at last so slighted and neglected by Lauderdale, (then become his enemy,) that he was necessitat to return home, without place or pension. Although his father and he computed their losses to be then (per lucrum cessans & damnum emergens) a 1000 pounds sterling, the interest of which, by this time, would have amounted to a considerable sum. Now let the world judge, if it be not consonant to equity and reason, that the family of Barrass (being the posterity of the said Sir George Ogilvy and his lady) should have a real reward, according to the merit of such an heroic and noble action, and a full recompense of the damage they sustained thereby. And by what is above narrated, truth doth appear in its naked colours, without fear or favour of any, for the God of truth will not suffer it to be smothered, nor pass without its due commendation, and deserved reward.

And such a singular piece of loyalty, so prudently and faithfully performed, should be a motive to induce all honest-hearted Scotsmen, and good patriots in this, and succeeding ages, not only to pay a grateful acknowledgement to the memory of these renowned persons Sir George Ogilvy of Barrass, and Dame Elizabeth Douglas his lady, but also to look upon their posterity, as the representatives of those, to whom Scotland owes its unconquered Crown.

16 – WILLIAM OGILVY'S 'TRUE INFORMATION'.

The following document, written by William Ogilvy, does not appear to have been published. Again, it presents his own version of his father's story:

'A True Information of the Honours of Scotland and the manner of their preservation in time of the English overrunning Britain and Ireland under Cromwell the usurper.'

Before his late Majesty King Charles the 2nd (of ever blessed memory) his going up to Worcester with the Scots army, the late Sir George Ogilvy of Barrass (then George Ogilvy) was made Governor of Dunnottar and had the crown, sword and sceptre of this kingdom entrusted to his custody there. He finding the said castle disappointed of men, ammunition and all other provisions, which his Majesty had ordered to be given in to it, and also perceiving the enemy prevailing over all, and all other forts reduced under their power and command save the said castle, then last of all his Majesty's dominions unrendered-up. And so perceiving himself destitute as aforesaid, and unable to hold out longer against an enemy at that time invincible, thought if he could preserve the Honours, he did all could be done, and what was of most concernment.

Whereupon he being a prudent man, considers that he would be forced to surrender the castle, and to give an account of the said Honours, whereupon he told his wife (being the daughter of Mr John Douglas of Barrass, brother-german to William Earl of Angus, grandfather of the late William Duke of Hamilton) who was also very prudent and of an undaunted courage according to her sex, that he could not longer hold out and therefore desired her to convey-off secure the Honours without his privity and knowledge, lest he being put to it, and exercised with torture might not know to declare where they were.

So she sends for Mr James Grainger's wife, and recommends to her care and fidelity the securing of them in the Church of Kinneff and that she might the more freely undertake and keep secret the matter the said Sir George's wife did engage and promise for herself and in name and behalf of her husband (though without his knowledge) to the said Mr James Grainger's wife, and her husband to stand in the gap between them and all danger.

So the Castle was surrendered on honourable terms of capitulation, one of the Articles being to give up the Honours or give an rational account of them. These are the very words of the capitulation which Sir William Ogilvy of Barrass, the said Sir George's son, has by him. So to be brief, after the Castle was surrendered up to the English, they desired the Honours or an account of them and the said Sir George told he knew not of them; his wife had sent them away and did not acquaint him where. Upon which the English distrust them and put the said Sir

George and his wife in strait prison in Dunnottar causing a sentinel to stand at the prison door, and another at the prisoners' bedside all night that they should not commune together about the Honours.

They were brought out and examined often, and still Sir George said his wife had sent them away without his knowledge, but where, he could not tell upon oath. His wife was next examined and she did boldly affirm that she delivered them to John Keith (now Earl of Kintore) who was then abroad at his travels, and knew not in the least of the securing and preserving of the Honours, nor what was become of them or the castle either. And she said that John Keith had delivered them to King Charles the 2nd at the Hague but the English, still distrusting them, kept them in a squalid prison in Dunnottar about twelve months. And also, during their imprisonment, a party of English were sent out to Barrass under cloud of night to apprehend and bring in the said Sir George and his wife's only son and child (who yet lives and was then but a young boy) with a design to afflict and to treat him inhumanely in sight of his parents, to extort, thereby, confessions from them but, by the Divine aid and Providence, he escaped a little (yea some minutes) before the soldiers came to the house of Barrass where he was, and underwent much toil and fatigue by travelling night and day in a slovenly habit and that under covert of a chapman's apprentice, till he got to his friends in Angus among whom he was concealed and kept. The chapman's name with whom the said Sir George's son went away (in occulto) is John Duncan who is yet alive in the parish of Arbuthnott, and shire of the Mearns.

And after the said Sir George and his wife had been imprisoned about twelve months, the English not being able to get a farther account of the Honours from them, upon mediation of friends, General Deane granted them liberty to go to their own house upon a bond of 2000 pounds sterling and the Laird of Morphie cautioner to enter them prisoners upon demand and that they should not go above three miles from their own house of Barrass without a pass, under which restraint they remained all the time till King Charles the 2nd's restoration. And all this time they had a special care of the Honours and sent, monthly, clean linen to Mr Grainger's wife with instructions to take them up and wrap them therein when the old linen was rotten lest they should have been spoiled or tarnished with dust and rust, they being hid and reposited in the west end of the said Church of Kinneff under forms or seats where the commonality sit. And the minister Mr James Grainger and his wife being still privy and the keepers of them there (according to the said Sir George's wife's order) and were faithful in their secrecy till his said late Majesty's Restoration and the said minister did redeliver the said honours to the said Sir George and he, according to order, did deliver them to the then Earl Marschall and got his receipt of them which was produced to his said late Majesty.

But notwithstanding this noble good service faithfully performed by the said Sir George and his wife as verily and really as 'tis here written, yet at his Majesty's restoration the then old Countess of Marschall wrote to his Majesty that her son, John Keith, had preserved the Honours of Scotland, being that the said Sir George had (unwarily) imparted to the Countess where they were hid, and how, by laying the blame on her son he had saved himself and concealed them from the English. So the said Sir George not knowing that the said Countess had taken occasion to allege and pretend any such thing, or that she had written to the King entrusts his affair to the then Earl Marschall to represent it to his said late Majesty and to get him a suitable reward.

But how soon the said Earl and his brother were at London, Kintore got the late Earl of Middleton to dissuade the Earl Marschall from acting for the said Sir George, and to act for his brother, to make him a great man, being it was Sir George's evasion, when questioned by the English, that the said John Keith (now Earl of Kintore) had them over seas to his said late Majesty, as is before at length expressed. Whereupon the said Earl Marschall was laid aside from naming the said Sir George's good service and his wife's, or their sufferings on that account, nor yet the due way and relation of the preservation of the said Honours.

And so with influence (as the supposed preserver of them) he was made Sir John Keith, Knight Marschall of Scotland, and got 400 pounds sterling of yearly pension which is yet settled upon and continued to one of his sons with the said place and title. So Sir George having followed the said

Earl Marschall up to court, and finding his affair there altogether wrong, represented the true state thereof, and the wrong was done him therein, to the late Earl of Airlie (then Lord Ogilvy) whereupon the said Earl represents to his said late Majesty, and the then Earl of Lauderdale, the wrong that the said Sir George was like to sustain by the Earl Marschall's neglecting of his affair, and thereby to frustrate him of his deserved reward and then the Earl of Lauderdale advised his said late Majesty to cause the honours be delivered to the Earl Marschall and to get his receipt upon them. For Lauderdale said if Sir John Keith had kept them Sir George was not able to get them, but if the said Sir George had the keeping of them 'twould evidently and undeniably appear who was verily the preserver of them.

But, in the meantime, the then old Countess of Marschall was earnestly soliciting and dealing with the said Mr James Grainger Minister of Kinneff to have the Honours (then hid with his privity and knowledge in the said church) delivered to her, but her design was rendered abortive, for Sir George having a surmise of it went forthwith and took up the sceptre out of the said church, and got an obligement from the said Minister to make the rest of the Honours forthcoming to him. And so after that the order was sent to the said Sir George to deliver them to the Earl Marschall, which he accordingly did and got his receipt on them and brought it up to his said late Majesty and Lauderdale who acknowledged it to be (as truly it is) the said Earl Marschall's hand writing. And after his Majesty's reading of it, the said Sir George humbly requested it back to be kept in his family as an evident and videmus of his loyalty and good service done to the King and kingdom of Scotland.

17 – MEMORIAL FOR THE EARL OF KINTORE PRIOR TO PRIVY COUNCIL ACTION.

This, following, is the Earl of Kintore's account submitted to the Lord Advocate in 1702 prior to the Privy Council process for libel against George Ogilvy:

When King Charles the Second went to England with the Scottish army, by his order the Crown, Sceptre and Sword were transported to the castle of Dunnottar to be under the care of the Earl Marschall who was allowed a lieutenant and some soldiers for the defence of the place. The Earl employed George Ogilvie, his servant, who being bred and born under him, the said George's father being porter in Dunnottar and never advanced to further degrees of service, yet his son being educated with the Earl was much in his favour and gave him commission to be his lieutenant when the King went to England.

In anno 1651 the Earl Marshall put the Honours at Dunnottar in the best posture he could and lodged the Honours in a secret place in the castle. But he being, in commission with the Earls of Crawford, Glencardin and others, met at Alyth with many of the King's friends there to consult about the affairs of the nation and government. But he with others were surprised and made prisoners by Colonel Alured. And, finding that he was to be carried to London, sent private orders to the Countess of Marschall, his mother, to take care of the Honours. And accordingly the Countess, having received the key, she went to the place where the Honours were and delivered them to George Ogilvie, the lieutenant, to care for them.

Although the Committee of Estates had ordered the Lord Balcarres to receive them out of Dunnottar, yet by the good conduct of Mr John Keith, now Earl of Kintore (when very young) and George Ogilvy's earnest desire, who was afraid to deny the Committee's order, did take upon him to refuse the giving them up to the said Lord Balcarres, which fell out very happily, for if they had been given out they had been undoubtedly seized upon, the English being then master of all Scotland.

Then the English, marching northward, the Countess's fears about the Honours increased, and therefore she ordered they should be privately carried off and an account sent to her where they were lodged. Some few days thereafter, the minister of Kinneff is put upon the contrivance, who managed it very faithfully, his wife and her maid having carried the Honours in bundle of flax to her own house, thereafter lodged them in church, and gave the Countess of Marschall a receipt bearing the places where they were lodged.

The English thereafter having besieged it, Dunnottar was surrendered upon a very base capitulation, as can be instructed, and the lieutenant was bound to deliver the Honours or give a rational account of them. And accordingly when they were required, George Ogilvy and his wife asserted that they were carried abroad by the now Earl of Kintore, then Mr John Keith, and delivered to the King in Paris, but George wanting documents, he and his wife were detained prisoners till the Earl sent a declaration from France, upon which they were set at liberty on bail.

The Earl of Kintore having then acknowledged under his hand the having of the Honours, and knowing the difficulties that might attend him if he should fall in the hands of his enemies, he stayed abroad till General Middleton came over to Scotland, and thereafter followed him over to Scotland. He endured a great many hardships, being taken in his landing in the Ely in Fife but, being in disguise as a young merchant lad, the English let him go. Thereafter coming north he corresponding with the Marquise of Montrose who had married his cousin german and, having got some friends with him, went to the hills and joined General Middleton and remained still there till they were defeated at Lochgarioch.

And when there was no further hopes left, he fell upon a contrivance of getting a receipt from General Middleton as if the Honours had been delivered to him at Paris by the King's order. And then the Countess of Marshall, by the mediation of friends, prevailed with General Monck to include him in the Marquis of Montrose's capitulation. And being challenged by Colonel Cobbet, then governor of Dundee, who was appointed by Monck to concert the articles of capitulation with the Marquis of Montrose, the said Cobbet told the Earl of Kintore, then Mr John Keith, that he was ordered by General Monck to inquire of him if he did carry the Honours abroad, which he owned, and upon production of General Middleton's receipt he was included in the capitulation with the Marquis, neither was there ever any further enquiry made about them till the King's restoration.

Then the Countess of Marschall wrote to the King to receive his Majesty's commands about the honours. By a very kind letter from his

Majesty, with thanks for her good service, she was desired to deliver them to the Earl Marshall, and as a mark of his Majesty's favour he not only made the Earl Lord Privy Seal, but gave also to Mr John Keith, now Earl of Kintore, the patent of Knight Marshall with a considerable fee for the said office. And thereafter he was created Earl of Kintore, and both these patents, amongst his other signal services, mention the preservation of the Honours, and the Lord Lyon is appointed to give him the Crown, Sceptre, and Sword, as an addition to his coat of arms.

Notwithstanding that the Honours were thus preserved the way and manner above mentioned, and that the King was sufficiently convinced thereof, and not only by his royal patents in favour of the Earl of Kintore, but by his private letters to the Countess of Marschall, acknowledged the same, yet the above said George Ogilvy, lieutenant, most impudently had the confidence to send up his son to London, arrogating to himself the sole preservation of the Honours, and having addressed the Lord Ogilvy, afterwards Earl of Airly, did introduce him to his Majesty. Upon which the Countess of Marschall sent up a gentleman express, and wrote to the Earl of Middleton a true information of the whole matter, which he very kindly represented to his Majesty, who refused to give ear to any such suggestions. And so his pretensions being defeated, there was no more of it.

Neither would the Countess of Marschall and the now the Earl of Kintore be dissatisfied with what favour the King might have bestowed on him. Nay, the Countess of Marschall, in a letter to his Majesty, did recommend the said George Ogilvy to his care. For it's not to be denied but that he knew the carrying of the Honours out of Dunnottar Castle and was kept prisoner for some time till the now Earl of Kintore, then Mr John Keith's, declaration from France of his having carried them abroad was the cause of the said George's liberation. But his impudent assuming the whole concern of their preservation to himself and thereby giving the lie both to his Majesty's patents and other clear documents, for instructing the truth of what is therein related.

It's to be observed that there being forty years past since the foresaid George Ogilvy's pretensions were frustrated, who lived a considerable time after the restoration, calmly though discontent, and that now this man, his son, should so long after raise new dust, to the most ignominious reproach and disgrace (by his printed pamphlet) of the memory of the Countess of Marshall and now Earl of Kintore. It's fit, therefore, my Lord Advocate advise how far the Earl of Kintore may have redress in this matter, and that Barrass may be pursued for printing, publishing, and dispersing of scandalous pamphlets, and that the Council will inflict a severe censure by fining and imprisoning his person, and burning of his prints.

18 – AN INFORMATION (FOR THE EARL OF KINTORE), 1702.

The following paper presenting the Earl of Kintore's case is especially interesting in that, unlike William Ogilvy's almost completely second-hand account, John, Earl of Kintore can presumably recall the truth of his own part in the events he details here.

An Information for the Earl of Kintore against Sir William Ogilvy of Barrass and David Ogilvy his son.

The Regalia of the Kingdom of Scotland were entrusted to the then Earl Marschall during the time of the late troubles, and were by the care of the late Earl, the Countess his mother, and especially by the prudence and firmness of John now Earl of Kintore, then Mr John Keith the Earl's brother, preserved from falling into the hands of the English, and after the restoration of King Charles the second, discovered and restored to the Government, with an ingenuous and honest account how they had been preserved, not omitting what concern Ogilvy of Barras (who was the Earl's lieutenant of the castle of Dunnottar, by a commission from the Earl himself) had in the matter.

But Sir George Ogilvy of Barrass, conceiving that it might be a great advancement for his family, if he were understood to be the sole preserver of the Honours, and that in a matter so mysterious and secret, it would be easy to assert boldly, did therefore ungratefully and foolishly set up for the honour of having done that service to his Majesty and the nation, without any assistance of the family of Marschall. But the thing being then recent and all the people alive who knew the circumstances, which served to give light to the truth, Barrass let fall his pretensions, and the true account of the preservation of the Crown, Sceptre and Sword, has not been brought in question by anybody for 40 years.

But in Anno 1701, there was a pamphlet printed and dispersed entitled, 'A True Account of the Preservation of the Regalia of the Kingdom of Scotland, Viz. the Crown Sword and Sceptre, from falling into the hand of the English Usurpers, by Sir William Ogilvy of Barrass, Knight and Baronet,' with the blazon of that family, and wherein he pretends to arrogate the chief merit of preserving the Regalia to Sir George Ogilvy of Barrass, his father, and to his mother, detracting at the same time from the Family of Marschall, and particularly alleging, that the Countess Dowager of Marschall, mother to this Earl had suppressed the truth, and imposed upon King Charles 2nd and that the Earl of Kintore was abroad, and knew nothing of the matter. The Earl has therefore raised a complaint before the Lords of Privy Council, against Barrass's elder and younger for this false defamatory libel. And to the effect, that the Lords of Privy Council may be fully informed concerning the preservation of the Regalia, and that the Earl may be vindicated, and Barrass's falsehoods discovered, the Earl begs liberty to make a true and ingenuous narration.

King Charles the 2nd being obliged to leave Scotland upon the prevailing of the English gave a Commission to the Earls Crawford, Marschall and others to manage the Government, and the Earl of Marschall having obtained an establishment for a garrison in the Castle of Dunnottar, he did name George Ogilvie, thereafter Sir George Ogilvy of Barrass, to be his lieutenant, as not doubting but he would be trustee to him, seeing the said George Ogilvy's Father, had been the Earl's porter, and the said George himself had been bred up about his family, and had received by the Earl's favour the first advance towards his better fortune.

The Earl of Marschall having got the Regalia, did deposit them in a secret place of the Castle of Dunnottar, of which he kept the key himself. But the Earl Marschall being surprised and taken by the English at Eliot

[Alyth], sent the keys of the place where the Honours were kept, to the Countess Dowager his mother, a person of great virtue, prudence, and loyalty, who came herself to Dunnottar, and delivered the Honours to George Ogilvie, with special order to take care of them, in case he should be forced to surrender the Castle.

About this time the Committee of Estates, seeing the English like to carry all before them appointed the Honours to be delivered to the Earl of Balcarras, which the said George Ogilvy was ready to have complied with, but was dissuaded by the present Earl of Kintore who at that time, although very young, did project a far more effectual way to preserve the said Honours, and indeed if the Honours at that time had been sent through the Country, which was full of the enemy's troops, or even had been delivered to the Committee of Estates which was shortly afterwards dissipate, they would have undoubtedly fallen into the hands of the enemy.

The English approaching to Dunnottar, and there being no appearance of relief, the said George Ogilvy gave the Honours to Mr James Granger minister of Kinneff who carried them out of the castle, and the said Mr James sent his wife to receive them, who by her maid did carry them away, being packed up in a burden of flax, and thereby they were brought safe to the minister's house, albeit they met with a party of the enemy upon the road, and were by the minister hid in holes dug under the pavement of the church, and as the trust was entirely from the Countess of Marschall in absence of the Earl who was then prisoner, so Mr James Granger gave a declaration to the Countess, written with his own hand, bearing date, the 31st of March 1652 acknowledging the custody, and describing the very places of the church where the Honours were hid and concluding in these words, 'that if it should please God to call me by death before they be called for, your Ladyship will find them in that place.'

But the better to cover this and to amuse the English, the Earl of Kintore, then Mr John Keith retired secretly and went to Paris where King Charles was, and then it was given out, that he had carried the Regalia beyond seas to the King. And when the Castle of Dunnottar was taken by the English, and Ogilvy detained prisoner until he should give an account of the Regalia, Ogilvy alleged for himself, that Mr John Keith had carried them beyond seas; and to support this story, a letter was procured from Mr John owning that he had done so, upon which Ogilvy was liberated.

King Charles 2nd having sent the Earl of Middleton to command in Scotland, the Earl of Kintore resolved to venture his life for his Majesty, and came along with him, and when that attempt proved unsuccessful, and that those who had been in arms for the King at that time were forced to capitulate, the Earl of Kintore foreseeing that he would be brought in danger for the Regalia, took from the Earl of Middleton a Receipt for the Regalia, as if they had been delivered by the Earl of Kintore to the Earl of Middleton at Paris, although it was truly dated at Keppoch.

The thing happened as the Earl of Kintore had foreseen, for he was taken up and examined strictly by Colonel Cobbet governor of Dundee who by General Monck's order did capitulate with the Marquis of Montrose and him, but having produced the receipt, and answered firmly and consistently, he was dismissed, and by these means the Regalia were no farther heard of, nor sought after till the Restoration.

After the Restoration, the Countess of Marschall gave a plain account of the whole matter ingenuously, owning Barrass's part as a servant under the Earl of Marschall, and which was no more than that Barras had once the keeping of the Honours, and delivered them to Grainger, and that he did not discover Grainger when he was examined by the English. Nor did the Countess forget Mr Grainger's fidelity in the matter, which did not at all diminish her own and the Earl of Kintore's merit, who were the principal actors and managers, and who projected the manner of preserving the Honours by lodging them in Graingers hands, and took his declaration concerning them, and by a very wise and prudent device, led the enemy off from the pursuit of the Honours, albeit that device did both expose the Earl of Kintore in his person and fortune, and his Majesty King Charles 2nd was so far convinced of the Earls good service, that he was pleased at that time to create him Knight Marschall, upon the narrative of the service done in preserving the Crown, etc.

But George Ogilvy of Barras had laid the design, to have the sole merit of preserving the Honours ascribed to himself and, for that end, endeavoured to persuade Mr Grainger that his fidelity in that matter was not represented to the King, but that the Countess of Marschall and her son, were taking the glory of the action entirely to themselves, and the only way to prevent it was, to deliver the Honours to Ogilvie, that he might have them to show and Ogilvy was to make a representation for himself and Mr Grainger to the King. Mr James Grainger being half persuaded by Ogilvy's misrepresentation, and yet not fully trusting him, granted him only a part of what he asked, having delivered the Sceptre to the said George Ogilvy of Barrass, retaining the rest, but however he took Barrass's receipt for the whole, which receipt was qualified by a back-note given by the minister to Barrass, whereby he acknowledges that albeit he had Ogilvy's receipt for the Honours, yet Ogilvy had got no more but the Sceptre, and obliges himself to make the rest forthcoming at demand, which back-note Barras has published in his Pamphlet.

Barrass having, by these means, in appearance the Honours at command, and having his son in London to solicit his business, under the favourable protection and countenance of the Lord Ogilvie, did boldly give it out, that he and his lady were the principal keepers and preservers of the Honours, and procured an order to himself to deliver them to the Earl Marschall, hoping that if the Honours were so delivered as he might have a receipt, it would confirm the story that he was the principal keeper and preserver of the Honours. And this order being transmitted by the son to George the father, George Ogilvy sent it to Mr Grainger, to go alongst with him to deliver up the Honours to the Earl Marschall, which he absolutely refused, having been abused by him before, and so went out of his house with the Crown and Sword to be delivered to the Earl Marschall, which George Ogilvy perceiving, met the minister on the road, with the Sceptre, and both came to Dunnottar at the same time, and accordingly delivered the Honours to the Earl Marschall in presence of the Viscount of Arbuthnott and several others. But George having been lieutenant of Dunnottar, and having had once the custody of the Honours from the Earl and Countess of Marschall, did propose to the

Earl Marschall that he might have a receipt, under the specious pretext as being necessary for his exoneration. And having got this receipt from the Earl, he immediately transmits it to his son at London, who improves it as a proof that his father had been the principal keeper and preserver of the Honours. And he procured a patent to be Knight Baronet, with a Charter changing the holding of his Lands, &c.

But all these being false representations, imposing upon his Majesty, and detracting from the good service done by the Earl of Kintore were quickly discovered, and Grainger who had been abused amongst the rest, gave an account in a letter to my Lady Marschall, yet extant, of Barrass's conduct with him, and the Countess of Marschall, and the Earl of Kintore having also complained, and redargued Barrass his false accounts by the writs abovementioned, Barrass let his pretensions fall, not only because he was redargued from the writs, but that the Earl of Middleton, the English officers who had examined anent the Honours in the time of the usurpation, and the Viscount of Arbuthnott, and the other persons who were present, when Mr Grainger as well as Barrass were all alive, were ready to have confounded Barrass his false and arrogant pretence.

But now Sir William Ogilvy his son presuming that the obscurity by the length of time, and death of many worthy persons who knew the circumstances of the matter, may favour his claim, has revived what his father first fraudulently contrived and fraudulently dropped, and endeavours by the forecited pamphlet, to insult the memory of the deceast Countess Dowager of Marschall, and detract from the merit and services of her son the Earl of Kintore, contrary to the truth itself, and contrary to the evidences abovementioned. But the Earl has the happiness to have the matter decided by his Majesty, in his letters patent to him as Knight Marschall, and by a letter under King Charles 2nd his hand to the Countess of Marschall, and another from the Earl of Middleton, wherein Barrass is treated as a little fellow, and by a patent creating his Lordship Earl upon the narrative of that very service, long after Barrass his arrogant pretensions, with a prescription of 40 years.

The Earls merit in this matter being vindicate by the narrative abovementioned, Barrass pamphlet with his pretensions upon that account, to have been the sole keeper and preserver of the Honours, falls in consequence. But because the pamphlet does not only advance matters false, but represents them in a way injurious to the Earl of Kintore and in a further vindication handed about in writing by the same Barrass, he insists farther upon the same falsehoods and injuries, the Earl has raised the foresaid libel before the Lords of Privy Council, and shall make the following observations upon the pamphlet.

And First, by the pamphlet it is evident, that Barrass his concern about the Honours was only as a servant, entrusted by the Earl Marschall, in as far as his commission to be lieutenant of Dunnottar was only from the Earl himself.

2) The Story as it is told by Barrass, of his Mothers conveying the Honours out of the castle without his fathers knowledge, and that this was by his fathers own contrivance, is little better than a jest.

3) Not to enter upon the question, whether Barrass maintained the castle of Dunnottar as long as it might have been kept out, or of the capitulation without extremity whereby he delivered up not only the castle, but the furniture and other goods belonging to the Earl Marschall and others, to a very considerable value, was honourable, it seems strange and disingenuous that Barrass should have capitulated upon the terms of delivering up the Crown, which yet he knew was not in his power.

4) The narrative pages seven and eight, alleges that the Lady Barrass, being examined concerning the Honours, pretended that the Earl of Kintore had carried them abroad to the King, and yet page eleven the same pamphlet alleges, that the Earl during the transactions was abroad at his travels, and knew nothing of the matter.

5) In the tenth page he asserts, that Captain George and his lady, were the principal keepers and preservers of the Honours whatsoever others pretend, and the only sufferers therefore, and in the eleventh page he adds, that the Countess of Marschall wrote to his Majesty, that her son John Keith now Earl of Kintore had preserved the Honours, being that he the said Captain George had unwarily imparted to her where they were hid, and that upon the said misrepresentation, her son was first created Knight Marschall, and thereafter Earl of Kintore, with a pension

for his pretended preservation of the Honours. Albeit by the minister's receipt it is clear and evident, that upon lodging the Honours in the Kirk of Kinneff, he gave the receipt and declaration to the Countess of Marschall bearing the particular places where they were hid. So that Captain George nor his Wife never imparted the same to the Countess. And not only thereby asserts what is false in that matter, but adventures even to belie his Majesty's Patents.

6) By a paper handed about in write, he asserts that he and his lady were the only sufferers for, and preservers of the Honours, and in the third page thereof asserts that 'Sir George his lady's making use of the now Earl of Kintore's name, was a very lawful stratagem in her, and that which no generous man abroad would have declined to own, But would not have reaped the fruits of Sir George and his Lady's Labours, nor taken the whole reward due for their Sufferings.' And in the last page thereof adds, that by his Narrative 'Truth doth appear in its naked Colour, without fear or favour of any'; which is not only an aggravation of his former bold assertions and falsehoods, but upon the matter a defiance to any one who would contradict them. And besides if (as Barrass grants) the Earl of Kintore owned the carrying away of the Honours, then it follows, that what he advances in his pamphlet, page eleven, is false viz. – that the Earl was abroad, and knew nothing of the matter.

7) This paper of his seems to be inconsistent with itself for it ascribes the sole preservation of the Honours to his own conduct: and yet in the third page of his written paper says that his Lady did not discover to him where the Honours were, till she was on deathbed, and then did impart to him how and where the Honours were hid and reposed, and took his hand upon oath, not to betray the trust she had committed to him. By which it is evident that the Minister made only the Countess Marschall known to the Place where the Honours were hid, which is documented by his receipt and declaration to the Countess. And Barrass has nothing but his own bare assertion to support his lady's knowledge and discovery made by her to him on deathbed.

8) Sir George seems to acknowledge by his own papers, that the King himself was convinced that it was arrogance in Sir George Ogilvy to

ascribe to himself the sole preservation of the Honours, for in the sixth page of his own paper, he says that when the Lord Ogilvy did solicit Strafford to represent the eminent services due by the said Sir George and his lady in preserving the Honours of Scotland, that the King's answer was, 'By my Lord Ogilvy's good leave it most not be so, for my Lady Marschall wrote to me, that she and her son John preserved the Honours.'

And, lastly, the receipt granted by the Earl Marschall, does not prove for Barrass that he had the keeping of the Honours but on the contrary, the back note granted by Mr Granger the minister to Barrass, joined with the Earl's Receipt, evince the contrivance on Barrass part; for to what end did Barrass give a receipt of the whole Honours, when he received only the Sceptre, if that simulation was not intended to be a false evidence that Barrass had the keeping of the whole. Or if ever Barrass had got the rest of the Honours from Mr Granger, is it to be thought that Granger would not have retired his back note in a matter of such consequence. But seeing Barrass had laid so many plots to have the appearance of being the keeper of the Honours, when he was not; it follows plainly, that the Earl Marschall's receipt was only intended by the Earl Marschall as an exoneration to Barrass of the trust he had of the Honours when he was lieutenant of Dunnottar, but Barrass out of a fraudulent design, took care to have the receipt so worded, as might best suite his purpose.

By all which its clear and evident: 1. That what was done by George Ogilvy in relation to the Honours was by commission and trust from the Earl of Marschall. 2. That the Countess delivered the Honours to him out of her own hand, with particular orders about their preservation. 3. That the Earl of Kintore kept the Honours from being given up to the Lord Balcarras, when he demanded them by order of the Estates. 4. That the Honours were carried out of the castle, and kept by the minister of Kinneff by the Countess direction during the usurpation. 5. That the Earl of Kintore by his letter from Paris, took upon himself all the danger, by owning that he had carried the Honours abroad, that upon that account he was upon the matter banished, and upon his return apprehended, and after his escape hunted from place to place, that he gallantly hazard his life under Middleton, that he wisely contrived the getting that general's receipt, which entirely quieted the English, that he underwent many hardships before capitulating, that he behaved with so much conduct and exactness, that he entirely secured the Honours from all further pursuit; And lastly, that Barrass these forty years bygone, was so far convinced of all this, that it was never attempted till of late by this Barrass or his son, to call the same in question. In respect whereof, and that Barrass printed paper is a most injurious defamation and atrocious slander to the truth, to his Majesty King Charles the 2nd's acknowledgements, and to the faith of repeated patents, it's hoped your Lordships will not only ordain him to retract the same, as a manifest villainy, but also will ordain the foresaid ignominious pamphlet to be burned by the hand of the hangman, and all other reparation made to the Earl of Kintore of his honour, fame, and good name, that can be proper against such injurious and reproachful undertaking, and will punish Barrass in his person and goods, as your Lordships shall think fit.

[Papers appended to the above, all previously introduced]
The King's Letter to the Countess Marschall, 1655.
Minister of Kinneff's receipt to the Countess Marschall, March 31, 1652.
The King's Letter to the Countess Marschall, 4 September 1660.
Declaration of James Granger minister at Kinneff concerning the Honours.
Letter from James Granger to the Countess Marschall, 12 November 1660.
The Earl of Middleton's Letter to the Countess Marschall, 15 November 1660.

19 – OGILVY'S ANSWERS TO KINTORE'S 'INFORMATION'.

Answers to, with remarks upon, a scurrilous paper called 'An Information' given be the said Earl of Kintore to the Privy-Council of Scotland, anno 1702, against the late Sir William Ogilvy of Barrass and David Ogilvy his son.

1) 'Tis alleged in that paper called An Information that especially by the prudence and firmness of John, Earl of Kintore, then Mr John Keith, the Honours of Scotland were preserved from falling into the hands of the English and after the restoration of King Charles 2nd discovered and restored to the government with an ingenuous and honest account how they had been preserved. But Sir George Ogilvy of Barrass, conceiving that it might be a great advancement for his family if he were understood to be the sole preserver of the Honours, and that in a matter so mysterious and secret it would be easy to assert boldly, did therefore ungratefully and foolishly set up for the honour of having done that service to his Majesty and the nation without any assistance of the family of Marschall; but the thing being then recent, and all the people alive who knew the circumstances which served to give light to the truth, Barrass let fall his pretensions, and the true account of the preservation of the honours was not called in question by any body for 40 years.

To which its answered that the late John, Earl of Kintore, doth acknowledge that the Regalia of the Kingdom of Scotland were entrusted to the then Earl Marschall during the time of the late troubles, and that they were by the care of the late Earl the Countess his mother, and especially by his prudence and firmness preserved from falling into the hands of the English &c. by which word especially (being very emphatic) the said John, Earl of Kintore, seems to assume to himself the greatest part in the preservation of the honours, thereby detracting from his brother, the then Earl Marschall's merit.

In anno 1674 the late Sir William Ogilvy of Barrass, son of the said Sir George, went up to London in expectation of the reward and pension promised to his father, but the then Secretary, being made his great enemy and a fast friend to the said Earl of Kintore, and he the said Earl, as he confessed to Mr Nisbet at Edinburgh, did make Sir William as many enemies as possibly he could at court, so that Sir William having so many and great enemies was shifted off and postponed, and at last wearied out that he was obliged after great loss of his time and money to return home without pension, place, or any pecunial reward, and his father Sir George reflecting upon his own and his lady's great losses and sufferings, and after all to see his son disregarded and himself unrewarded for his faithful and discreet service, as the said Earl of Kintore in his libel expresses it, he, Sir George, contracted melancholy and dyed sometime thereafter. All which proves that he was not satisfied with that part of his reward he at first got, neither did he let fall his pretensions but expected a pension as the King had promised him.

This doth also cut off Kintore's pretension and allegation of prescription. And although such an interruption and litiscontestation had not been made in anno 1674 yet, by the civil-law and according to equity and reason vitiosa possessio non juvat possidentem et quod ab initio non valet non potest tractu temporis convalescere. And though the said Earl of Kintore taxes the said Sir George as having ungratefully and foolishly set up for the preserver of the Honours &c yet he ought rather to have gratefully and prudently as well as justly acknowledged Sir George his lady's act of kindness (having been the greatest ever was done him by any) in making use of his name as a means, though it proved but a small one, to conceal the honours from the enemy. I say the said Earl of Kintore was in point of gratitude bound to have had a singular regard for the family of Barrass being the posterity of that lady and to have promoted and advanced their honour and interest, since she gave the first rise to his grandeur and estate. But to wrong, oppress, and maltreat the family of Barrass, so much as the said Earl of Kintore has done, was barbarous ingrate and inhumane.

2) The said Earl of Kintore Alleges in his printed information that George Ogilvy, when Governor of Dunnottar Castle, was afraid to deny the order of the Committee of Estates anent transporting and securing of the honours and that he, the said Earl, did dissuade him and that he the said Earl did refuse to give out the honours out of the said Castle to Balcarras having projected a more effectual way to preserve them; and that if they had been delivered to the said Committee, which was shortly thereafter dissipated, they the honours had undoubtedly fallen in the hands of the enemy; and that he, the said Earl, though very young, apprehending the danger, refused to give the honours to Balcarras and he the said Earl of Kintore

did avert this, as if he had had any trust of the honours or concern with the keeping of the said Castle. And the said Earl alleges in his libel or Council letters that the honours having escaped this hazard were still kept in the said Castle, but the English marching northwards towards Dunnottar, the foresaid Committee ordered, the honours to be conveyed privately out of the way, which was done by the faithful assistance of one Mr James Grainger, minister of Kinneff. The said John Earl of Kintore, in his printed information, alleges that the English approaching Dunnottar, and there being no appearance of relief, the said George Ogilvy gave the honours to Mr James Grainger, Minister of Kinneff, who carried them out of the Castle and the said Mr James sent his wife to receive them.

Now let the world judge if the said Earl of Kintore his assertions anent his and his said mother's preserving the Regalia or honours of Scotland be not this far inconsistent and contradictory. The said Earl of Kintore alleges in his paper called An Information that the said Barrass was redargued by the writs (meaning the pretended letters and declarations from Grainger, the Minister). So far from any such thing neither the said Earl nor his mother the Countess of Marschall did ever allege or produce any such writs till this late process anno 1702 which, if they had had or thought probative or authentic it's unquestionable they would have made use of them when the minister and his wife were alive, especially when the said Earl's mother was very hard upon the said Sir George by many law-suits and expensive pleas before the lords of session by reason he would not say she and her said son had preserved the Regalia.

That the said Sir George held out Dunnottar Castle when governor there longer then the then Committee of Estates the Chancellor or Lord Balcarras did think probable nay possible is manifest by their letters aforesaid. And the said Earl of Kintore acknowledges in the account of his family to Mr Nisbet, that the said castle was not able to hold out long if once attacked and that when it was surrendered the English, finding the honours were withdrawn, threatened the greatest cruelty on the besieged. This is a further proof of Sir George's valour and gallantry and likewise of his and his lady's sufferings for the Honours who were the only persons challenged and imprisoned on that account, the rest of the garrison being dismissed after they had marched out honourably according to capitulation as aforesaid. And if Sir George and his lady had not been faithful and honest they might, through avarice, have sold the honours or, through timorousness, told the enemy where they were hid, and none in Scotland could have hindered them. But they were true to their trust and loyal to the utmost degree.

In that paper called a Declaration from Mr James Grainger, minister of Kinneff, to the then Countess of Marschall it's said that Grainger thought fit to declare that in August 1651, by the Countess of Marschall, the Honours were delivered to George Ogilvy of Barrass with charge to him to secure them, and he keeping them in Dunnottar till there was no loner probability of maintaining the castle, he employed me, having sufficient assurance of my loyalty and fidelity in promise keeping, to carry the honours out of the house and secure them.

In the first place it's questionable how Grainger could know anything relative to the said honours before they were entrusted to his wife, or that he had then any acquaintance of or concern with the Countess of Marschall. And, besides, the Earl Marschall's commission was given to the said Sir George with trust and command of the said castle, in July before, and that the trust of the honours was at the same time given to him is evident by the Earl Marschall's receipt, which plainly proves that the Earl Marschall, and none else did entrust the care keeping and preserving of the Honours to the said Sir George. And by Grainger's saying that the said Sir George Ogilvy employed him having experience of his fidelity in promise keeping &c., it's evident that the honours were not entrusted to Grainger by the said Countess, her contrivance or order, as is alleged.

And that pretended Declaration bears that Grainger granted a ticket to the said Countess of having the honours in his custody, but it makes no mention that he had them in trust from her ladyship (and if there had been any such ticket methinks it would have been produced at first). And Grainger adds that George Ogilvy had obtained a receipt from the then Earl Marschall and sent it or the double thereof to London to his son, as if the honours had been in his custody and by him preserved, although it be well known to his son that I had them in my house akeeping ever

since the first delivery of them to me. This pretended declaration is contradictory in itself, and also inconsistent with the tenor and purport of
Grainger's pretended receipt, wherein mention is made of several places
in the said Church where they, the Honours, are said to have been hid
and now alleging they were kept in the minister's house, it's plain the said
receipt and Declaration, as they are called, do clash one another and the
said pretended declaration being posterior to the Earl Marschall's receipt
of the honours to George Ogilvy it may shrewdly be suspected it was
elicit.

And as for Grainger's last letter to the Countess, really it doth not
appear to be the strain of language in the North of Scotland at that time,
for he begins 'I could not of duty omit to write to your ladyship at this
time for Barrass is now offering at high things namely to improve against
your ladyship &c.' And, besides, this letter is very reflective upon the
then Earl Marschall's honour, as if his lordship should have given the said
George Ogilvy a receipt of the honours the night before his Lordship
had received them which is both unreasonable and unjust to imagine.
And 'tis most certain if Grainger had delivered the Regalia to the Earl
Marschall by the Countess her order, or as having them in trust from
her ladyship, the Earl Marschall would have made mention thereof by a
clause in the said George Ogilvy his receipt or else have given Grainger
a particular receipt.

As to that pretence of the said Earl of Kintore's that, when the Earl of
Middleton came to Scotland to command a party for the King, he the
said Earl of Kintore joined him and got a receipt from him that he had
delivered the honours to the Earl of Middleton. At the defeat of that
party he the said Earl of Kintore was hardly put to it to tell where the
Honours were, to which 'tis said he answered that he had given them
to the Earl of Middleton and had his receipt thereon. And he says that
the English remained satisfied and gave over any further search for the
honours. Whereas Sir George Ogilvy and his lady's enlargement from
close prison being only obtained upon bail of 2000 lib: str. and they were
enforced to find bail of 500 lb. str. in the time of their confinement under
which Sir George's lady died and he continued therein 'till the King's

restoration and Sir George and his lady's enlargement was obtained upon bail as aforesaid by the mediation of friends, particularly James Ogilvy of Shannally, a cousin of Sir George's, to whose house Sir William, Sir George's son, fled for sanctuary from the fury of the enemy when his father and mother were prisoners in Dunnottar. I say, as their enlargement was only obtained ut supra, so their strict confinement and being always obliged upon advertisement to enter themselves close prisoners, during which they were frequently examined and their house of Barrass searched doth evidence and show that the Enemy were never fully satisfied anent the transporting and securing of the honours.

And some of that party Commanded by Middleton set fire to the entry of Sir George's house of Barrass and wounded him in the hand, which was mutilated to his death (he being then at liberty from close prison and confined to his house of Barrass before the defeat of that party), and consequently that frivolous pretence of the said Earl of Kintore's falls to the ground.

The said John, Earl of Kintore, having, as before mentioned given account of his family to Mr Alexander Nisbet, professor of heraldry at Edinburgh, to be printed in his book of heraldry, in which account the said Earl not only takes upon him the preservation of the honours of Scotland from falling into the hands of Oliver Cromwell but likewise throws several reflections on Sir George Ogilvy of Barrass his memory, besides the taking from him the glory of his fidelity and his noble service to his King and country, wherefore, the late Sir William Ogilvy being informed thereof was sensibly touched that such a reflective account should be published and handed down to future ages and thought himself obliged in honour and conscience to vindicate the memory and to perpetuate the integrity, loyalty and sufferings of his father and mother, and accordingly caused publish a true and impartial account of the preservation of the Regalia of Scotland, as aforesaid, upon the sight of which the said Earl of Kintore was extremely nettled to find the matter set in a true light and to see that his Lordship, though rewarded as the preserver of the Honours by being first made Knight Marschall and then nobilitate with a yearly pension of 400 lib. sterling.

I say, to see that he had no other part in that service than the owning what Sir George's lady said be way of evasion to sham the enemy, he, the said Earl, was so much incensed at the discovery that he laid hold on some expressions in the said account which the just resentment of the injury done Sir George Ogilvy and his family by the above mentioned paper given to Mr Nisbet had extorted. I say his Lordship upon these ingenuous and plain expressions founded a complaint to the Lords of his Majesty's Privy-Council of Scotland anno 1702 against the late Sir William Ogilvy of Barrass and his eldest son, the present Sir David Ogilvy of Barrass, alleging (with many cruel words) that they were guilty of defamation &c. Sir William Ogilvy being sick and not able to travel, having been valetudinary for many years before, sent up a certificate upon soul and conscience which his procurators gave in, and humbly expected that the lords of Privy Council would not have sustained any process against him until he had been able to come up for making his full defence, for they said that by the inviolable constitution of the forms of Council there can be no procedure against a party whose essionzy is relevantly made.

Yet the said Earl of Kintore's moyen [usu. means or method or, as in this case, influence] was such that the libel was read in absence, and the said account ordered to be burnt, which was accordingly done. Yet the said Earl's fury did not stop here, but he summoned Sir William and his son de novo, and Sir William was put to a double expense to a physician by renewing his certificate, and the said Earl had double his number of advocates, and Sir William's son, the present Sir David Ogilvy, did compear personally but had no friend to give the lords of Privy Council a full information of his case or a true account of what he had to say, and was so modest being assured of his innocence and designing to sweeten my Lord Kintore who had then so great interest and moyen that he gave in no defences and the then Earl Marschall, being well satisfied both of Sir William and his son's just intentions, did solicit the Earl of Kintore his uncle to let the process fall but he was inexorable, and Sir William's advocates told that his son, the present Sir David Ogilvy, never intended anything dishonourable to the family of Marschall or any injury to the Earl of Kintore, and when Sir David was desired to speak he said only these words 'I adhere thereto' meaning ut supra, and what now was spoke by the advocates qua advocates he does not own nor regard it.

And when he was obliged afterwards to compear before a committee of the Council he told my Lord Mar, who was praeces of that committee and my Lord Kintore's near relation, that whereas he understood that the words he lately spoke before the Privy Council were conceived in a sense far different from what he meant wherefore he craved leave to explain his meaning, being only this, that he never intended anything dishonourable to the family of Marschall nor yet any injury to the Earl of Kintore, and according to that rule in the Civil Law in ambiguous orationibus maxime spectanda est sententia ejus qui eas protulisset.

But he said that as for the preservation of the honours of Scotland by his grandfather and grandmother he would own and maintain the same so long as his blood was warm, and that they were great losers and sufferers by the doing thereof, and did by way of expostulation boldly ask what my Lord Kintore (who with his eldest son William, Lord Inverurie, now Earl of Kintore were sitting with the committee) did lose or suffer upon that account, and his words were that his owning of the matter was the means of Sir David's grandfather and grandmother's liberation from prison. 'Not so, My Lord,' said Sir David, ''Twas upon Sir Robert Grahame of Morphie's bail and bond of cautionry that they were liberated.' At which his Lordship was nonplussed. And these lords granted My Lord Kintore an uncommon favour which was to cause one of Sir David's Advocates and his only agent depone against him. This procedure gave him sufficient umbrage to think that the said Earl of Kintore would then worst and run him down and as the most liable and feasible way to prevent such treatment Sir David did the next Council day (when the committee was to make their report) present a petition to the Lord High Chancellor and the remaining Lords of her Majesty's Privy Council of Scotland, and for brevity's sake I shall only insert some paragraphs of it as follows:

'As to any expressions that may fall from a party when he is in extreme concern, as they are to be interpreted in the most benign sense, so his own explication of them is always received de recenti for exculpating the same from a delinquency. And your petitioner humbly craves leave to explain himself as to what he spoke before your lordships in Council,' his meaning being solely that he intended no injury to the Earl of Kintore nor anything dishonourable to the family of Marschall.

'It is most certain that neither advocate nor writer nor agent is bound to depone what is privately told them by their client otherwise it would be the most pernicious precedent and thereafter there should be no trust, wherefore your petitioner humbly craves to be assoilzied.' [absolved]

Notwithstanding all this, the Lords of Privy Council, not getting full information of the case nor a true account of what Sir David had to say in his defence, and my Lord Kintore being then a person of so great interest did so prepossess these lords that they fined this present Sir David Ogilvy of Barrass in a 100 lib. sterling and ordered him to be imprisoned during their pleasure, which hard sentence did enforce him to exert the principle of self preservation and to leave his native country for about twelve months (although his predecessors had done and suffered so much for the honour thereof) to the neglect and prejudice of his affairs and the concerns of his family (his father Sir William being superannuated and unable by long sickness to look after them) as well as the spending of his money and time unprofitably, when he might both have husbanded the one and employed the other at home. And the said John Earl of Kintore did raise letters of horning &c caption and adjudication and all manner of diligence against the said Sir David Ogilvy in his absence designing the ruin of his fortune, and adding affliction to his afflicted and aged parents.

As for the reflections the said Earl of Kintore casts upon Sir George Ogilvy's father though they are to be despised and, as all verbal injuries & personal reflections are esteemed worthy of nothing but neglect, yet it must be said that such opprobrious allegations foully and maliciously to bespatter the dead in spite to the living, plainly demonstrates the badness of one's cause, for he that hath no better weapon must throw dirt. And suppose that what the said John Earl of Kintore charges on the memory and reputation of Sir George and his father were true (as it is a manifest falsehood) yet it could not contribute to fortify his pretensions nor authenticate his cause. And besides it was most unmannerly and ungen-teel in a man of his quality to have recourse to lies, though with some they are sooner believed and go glibber down then truth, and 'tis the custom and practice of this wicked age in which it may be said ter-ras astrea reliquit to follow that devilish maxim of Matchivill (who was so well skilled in pseudo-policy) fortiter calumniare aliquid adhaeret or where truth is wanting to supply with calumnies and aspersions, and to blacken the fame of those they hate by heavy and disgraceful imputations on their memory, there being some men that, merely to gratify their ill nature, and like thorns that can do no other but scratch and tear, rake into the ashes of the dead, do scandalize the living, give a malicious turn to everything, and do blur the good names of those against whom they bear a grudge by injurious calumnies and spiteful libels.

And a libel is justly defined a bell with a lie tied to the end of it to ring the scandal up and down. Now although, as is said, the reflections cast by the said Earl of Kintore on Sir George's father be not worthy of regard, yet, to satisfy all the unbiased and unprejudiced, as well as to put a curb upon the foulmouthed, these considerations following are offered to the view of all.

1) If Sir George Ogilvy's father had been in such a base employment or of such a mean extract as the Earl of Kintore alleges, it is not to be thought that Sir John Douglas being the Earl of Angus brother's son would have consented to, far less signed, a contract of marriage (which is yet extant) between the said Sir George Ogilvy and his sister Elizabeth Douglas wherein Sir George's father takes burden upon him for his son and binds for such a conjunct fee as was correspondent to the tocher, being a competent sum in those days. The contract is dated the last day of January 1634.

2) Is it to be thought that William Earl Marschall would have used Sir George with so much familiarity and respect as belongs to a gentleman, which is evident by the Earl's missive letters ut supra? Can it be thought that that noble person would have treated Sir George Ogilvy in such a manner if he had been bred and brought up from a mean and obscure beginning by the Earl Marschall and in his family as the Earl of Kintore alleges?

And, besides, it's well known in the country and neighbourhood that both Sir George and his father lived creditably as gentlemen and were esteemed as such. And as a further proof of the confidence reposed by the family of Marschall in the said Sir George and his son the late Sir William, there's a letter yet extant from the late William Earl Marschall to the late Sir William Ogilvy of Barrass Dated at Inverugie, September 14th, 1702, wherein his Lordship says:

'Our family have always had you our friend and nothing can show it me more than that you'll heartily concur for the choosing such men to represent our shire as are of such good principles that greed will not bias nor threats frighten from their duty. So for the well you wish your Country and the friendship I expect from you I'm persuaded you will be for them. I am sorry to hear you have been ill for some time. I have a sedan at your service. The way is short and a little of the air may I hope do you good so makes no doubt of seeing you at our head court which will very singularly oblige Sir, your affectionate and humble servant, sic subscribitur, – Marschall'

And the said Sir William did, in obedience to his Lordship's desire, go to the head court and went seldom abroad afterwards. And it is to be observed that this letter was written by the Earl Marschall a little after and in the same year that the Earl of Kintore, uncle to the said Earl Marschall, did by his moyen and interest with the Privy Council of Scotland worst and run down the late Sir William Ogilvy and his son the present Sir David. As to the preservation of the Regalia of Scotland from falling into the hands of Oliver Cromwell, it doth evidently appear how and by whom that important matter was transacted, and for the late Sir William Ogilvy of Barrass to give an account thereof in defence of his said ancestors' memory and good name attacked as aforesaid, and by appearing truth's champion to countermine the subterfuges and wipe off the paint with which it was contaminated and varnished over could not be reckoned in the construction of law justice or reason any reproach injury or villainy with which the said Earl of Kintore taxes him frequently in his libel stuffed with calumnies slanders and detractions which seems to have proceeded from malice and to avenge the just disappointments he was then like to meet with (and which his family will now be sensible of) by the mere force and dint of truth which will sooner or later exert itself however by art or artifices it may be for a while concealed, and give to persons and actions the just praise or blame they deserve.

For justice ought to be rendered to every man's desert in speaking the naked truth, for truth never grows old, neither is there any respect to be paid to a greyheaded error, and there's so plain a line drawn between great truth and gross errors that it's visible to every capacity and an ordinary understanding that is not under a violent prejudice or blinded by some vice or fault of the will may easily discern. Men by speaking truth gain more credit in the world and have more peace in their consciences, for honesty and integrity is the best policy and the most effectual and lasting instrument of doing business, and Solomon well observes the lip of truth is established for ever and a lying tongue is but for a moment.

And they who write without vouchers, which has been the error of great historians, do often impose falsehoods for truth and if the error fall on things and actions they occasion great mischiefs. And without taking the method I've done 'twas not otherwise possible to unravel so many intricacies nor to set so many quite forgotten, at least misrepresented transactions and events, in their genuine light. And men have an undoubted assurance of matter of fact more ancient by far than these above related and the distance of them from our times creates no manner of scruple concerning them. That there was such a man as Alexander the Great and that he conquered Darius and the Persians, that Julius Caesar invaded England and in some measure subdued it, and that he overcame Pompeii in the Battle of Pharsalia, and innumerable other very ancient matters of fact are firmly believed without any matter of doubt and scruple by mankind notwithstanding they were done so long ago.

To return from this digression; I do now appeal to the candid reader if John Earl of Kintore had any better proofs either for his pretensions as the special preserver of the honours of Scotland or yet for his reflections and calumnies on Sir George Ogilvy and his ancestors then an ipse dixit, as is evident by what's above related all documented scripto.

20 – OGILVY'S ANSWERS TO THE COMPLAINT.

Answers for Sir William Ogilvy of Barrass to the Complaint raised against him by the Earl of Kintore, with concourse of Her Majesty's Advocate.

Sir George Ogilvy of Barrass, descended of the family of Airly, was in anno 1651 made deputy governor of Dunnottar, where the Honours, namely Crown, Sceptre and Sword, were deposited for safety. But the English prevailing, so as this was the only fort which did hold out, Sir George contrived the ensuring of the Honours in this manner. Having communicated his anxiety to his lady (who was a daughter of the Earl of Angus's brother) she causes convey them in a pack of tow out of the Castle to the Kirk of Kinneff where, by assistance of Mr Granger the minister, they were buried, and from time to time cured against spoiling. But all without Sir George's knowledge of the place lest torture might extort the discovering of it. For the castle, destitute of men and ammunition, being surrendered on honourable terms, one of the articles was, that Sir George should deliver up the Honours or give a rational account of them. But, on his declaring that he knew not where they were, his lady having taken them away, and thereupon, she being threatened with torture, for evading thereof said, that she had delivered them to John Keith (now Earl of Kintore) for carrying them abroad to the King, which the English distrusting, they were both committed close Prisoners for about a year, till released a little on bail of 2000 lib. sterling, and the restraint was continued till the lady died, and the King returned.

In Anno 1660s, Sir George (to whom his Lady before Expiring had told the secret) sends his son Sir William Ogilvie, the defender, to court, who presents a petition to the King, representing that his father had preserved the Honours with the hazard of his life, and under imprisonment, which occasioned the death of his wife, and seeing he could not desert that great charge of caring for them, had sent to know His Majesty's pleasure &c. Whereupon the King ordered them to be delivered to the Earl Marschall on his receipt.

And accordingly the Earl grants a receipt to Sir George, which acknowledges, that they were at first entrusted to him, which truth is further evidenced by: the Chancellors letter to Sir George, while the castle stood out, about delivering them to Balcarras; the narrative of General Dean's order about his commitment, and liberation upon bail; some letters by the minister to Sir George after the restoration, and the ministers delivering the Sceptre to him, and accepting a discharge from him; together with a letter from the King himself while at Paris; and another from Middleton; besides several other evidences in write; particularly the Kings narrative to Sir George's Charter changing the holding of his lands and his coat of arms from the Lyon Court, bearing a Lyon crowned with an Imperial Crown, holding in his dexter paw a Sword, with a Thistle in the dexter chief &c. With this Motto on an Escroll, Praeclarum Regi & Regno Servitium &c.

Though such an honourable merit might have been expected to have been the reaper of its own reward, yet that was disappointed, and Sir William after his father's decease sat still, till of late, the Earl of Kintore sent an account of his family to Mr Nisbet (who is writing a book of heraldry) wherein his Lordship not only ascribes to himself the sole preservation of the Honours, but likewise throws several dishonourable reflections upon Sir George's memory, besides the taking from him the glory of his fidelity, and his noble service to his King and country. About which juncture of time it was likewise reported that the like narrative was sent to be insert in Morerie's Dictionary.

Whence it is manifest, that any relation Sir William might have given of the state of the case, resolved into a proper self-defence of his fathers memory, and of the only reward that was left him, namely the honour of his family, and that by no more than telling the truth of a history, in so far as it did appear by adminicles in write; and, even this, no sooner than after he was attacked, as aforesaid.

Notwithstanding whereof, the Earl is pleased to raise a council complaint, alleging (with many cruel words) that the defender, in a late pamphlet, hath belied the pursuers patents &c. and concluding recantation and other punishments. To which it is answered in the general that as the defender had always a just veneration for the family of Marschall, so he never designed injury to the Earl of Kintore. And as he is not bound to know the contents of narratives in his Lordships patents, so he never advanced any more than the purport of authentic writes extant to be produced, and whereof an inventory is hereto annexed, the general contents whereof are compendized in the defenders charter, and coat armorial, above narrated, whence there can never a crime be inferred from telling a truth, especially, when it is not told, without necessity, but for making out a most natural and lawful self defence, which takes off all animus injurandi, and purges the presumption of offending.

In Particular (the complaint being held as represented) it is answered to the several members thereof as follows. (Denying always the libel, and qualifications thereof as libelled.)

1. There needs no notice to be taken of the assertion, that Sir George was brought up as a servant about the Earl of Marschall's family, for (though that could be no reproach) its known how he was a very well born gentleman, descended by his father from the Earl of Airly, and his lady descended from the house of Angus, And as the Earl Marschall's first commission to Sir George for his being a cornet designed him of Pitdovie, so the Second Commission for governor of Dunnottar, designs him of Barrass, besides many letters from the Earl, which do him the honour to bear several expressions of great intimacy and respect.

2. As to the main part of the libel itself, the same is not relevant, because the defender never did any thing with intention of defaming the complainer and what is necessary for his own self defence, either in honour or interest can never found a delinquency. And as to the particular qualifications thereof, it is plain, that Sir George had the keeping of the Honours, by the Earl of Marschall's own receipt acknowledging the same, and the other evidences above represented, and it neither is nor can be proven, that the complainers mother either had the key, of the place in which they were lodged or contrived the carrying off thereof. Nor is the defender concerned, what merits the complainer may claim, or are contained in his patents, for as the defender tells only the truth in his own vindication and in the defence of his father's memory, so he was not

obliged to know, nor has he as yet seen, what narratives are in the complainers patents. Whence there can be no crime upon that head.

Though Sir George, or his lady, did assert that the Honours were carried abroad by the complainer, for avoiding the cruelties threatened by the English against them, yet, ex obedientia facti, the Honours were never carried out of Scotland but, on the contrary, kept by Mr Granger in trust, first from Sir George his lady, and thereafter from himself which is manifest by the adminicles above mentioned. And this sufficiently clears, that whatever followed upon that supposition, which was no more than a color quaesitus does nowise prejudge the defender in the present Case.

The defender is as little touched, by the Kings conferring favours on the Earl of Marschall or the complainer, for all that is consistent with Sir George Ogilvy's personal fidelity, astructed beyond contradiction in manner above set down. And as to the other insinuations of the libel: that Sir George gave up the castle upon mean conditions, and that the defender has villainously traduced the complainer's honour and merit &c, its answered that, as the first of these does not concern the present case, so its most certain that Sir George was the last in Scotland that kept up arms for the King at that time. And as to the second, the complainers merits and honours are consistent with Sir George's, and its a rule both in law and nature, that what truth the defender tells ob propriam tutelam, id jure fecisse existimetur.

Though the defenders procurators do thus far informative represent a part of his case, yet its humbly hoped that her Majesty's High Commissioner, and the Lords of Council, being so far satisfied, both of the import and grounds of the cause, will not sustain any process against him, since he has a testificate upon soul and conscience, that he is not able to travel, until he be able to come up for making his full defence, for, by the inviolable constitution of the Forms of Council, there can be no procedure against a party, whose essoinzie [reason for absence] is relevantly made.

21 – PROCEEDINGS OF THE PRIVY COUNCIL AGAINST WILLIAM OGILVIE.

Proceedings of the Privy Council of Scotland in the cause, John Earl of Kintore against Sir William Ogilvy of Barrass, Knight – Edinburgh, the 8th July, 1702

Act in favour of the Earl of Kintore, for burning the book emitted by Barrass at the Cross, by the hands of the hangman.

About the libel or letters of complaint, purchased and raised before the Lords of Her Majesty's Privy Council, at the instance of John Earl of Kintore, Knight Marschall of this ancient kingdom of Scotland, with concourse of Sir James Stewart; her Majesty's Advocate, for Her Highness interest, in the matter underwritten: That where every man's honour ought to be dear to him as his life, and that an injury by way of defamation, in point of truth and honour, and tending to rob any person thereof, especially where his truth and honour is concerned as the most delicate and tender matters, is a most atrocious injury, not only most sensible in the person injured, but aiming to expose him in the view and construction of all men; and therefore, by the law of this and all other well-governed realms, most severely punishable.

Nevertheless, it is of verity that Sir William Ogilvy of Barrass, Knight, is guilty of the foresaid crime of defamation, and that in the most injurious and insolent manner, in so far as George Ogilvie, father to the said William, having been bred and brought up from a very low and obscure beginning by the deceast Earl Marschall, and in his family, and having, about the year 1651, been made lieutenant of the garrison of Dunnottar by the said Earl, the keeper of the said castle, by this means, the Honours of this said kingdom, viz. the Crown, Sceptre and Sword, which, by King Charles the Second, when at that time going for England, were committed to the said Earl, to be secured in the said Castle of Dunnottar, fell to be in some manner under the charge of the said Sir George, according to the trust the Earl had reposed in him.

But the Earl having lodged the Honours in a secret place of the castle, and thereafter coming to be unluckily surprised, with several other noblemen, at Eliot [Alyth], and with them made prisoners and carried to London, he was necessitated to send his private orders, with the key of that secret place where the Honours were, which he always kept about him, to the Countess of Marschall, his mother, praying her to take care of the Honours, it being no more in his power to look after them, whereupon, she entrusted them to the care and keeping of the said Sir George as lieutenant of the place as said is, who, though he received the said trust, yet in effect, had proved very unlucky in it.

If the said Earl of Kintore pursuer, then Mr John Keith, had not, albeit very young, by a happy foresight prevented the great hazard, in as much as when the Committee of Estates had, about that time, ordered the Lord Balcarras to receive the Honours out of the said Castle of Dunnottar, and the said Sir George was very much afraid to deny the Committee's order yet the said pursuer apprehending the danger, refused to give them out to the said Earl of Balcarras, which did very visibly, in the event, prevent their falling into the English hands. When, within a little thereafter, the English became masters of all Scotland, the Honours having thus escaped this hazard, were still kept in the castle.

But the English marching northwards towards Dunnottar, the foresaid Countess ordered the Honours to be conveyed privately out of the way, which was done a few days thereafter by the very faithful assistance of one Mr James Grainger, a minister at Kinneff; who by his wife and his maid caused bring the Honours, in a bundle of flax into his own house, and then lodged them in the church with a very exact caution, and gave the Countess Marschall a receipt bearing particularly the place of the kirk where they were hid, and which indeed was the security of the Honours, through the good conduct of the Countess, and the faithful service of the minister and his wife, during the whole time of the English usurpation.

For the English thereafter having besieged Dunnottar, it was surrendered by George Ogilvy, the lieutenant upon a very mean capitulation, and the lieutenant was thereby bound to deliver the Honours, or give a rational account of them. Whereupon, when Sir George and his wife were required, they asserted the Honours were carried abroad by the pursuer, and delivered to the King at Paris, which was indeed the contrivance that the complainer then advised, and the principal cause of his going abroad. But Sir George not having at that time got the Earl's declaration from Paris, he and his wife were kept prisoners until the Earl wrote home from Paris, owning that he had the Honours, and delivered them as said is, which proved the means of Sir George's liberation.

But the Earl having thus far concerned himself for the preservation of the Honours, he was constrained for to remain abroad, for fear of the English, until the Earl of Middleton came over to Scotland, and then the pursuer accompanied him in that expedition, in which he met with several hardships, being at first taken by the English, and then constrained to join with General Middleton and the rest in the hills, until they were all defeat. At which time the pursuer foreseeing his danger, fell upon a most happy contrivance both for the security of his own person and likewise for the safety of the Honours.

For General Middleton being to leave Scotland, the pursuer took a receipt of the Honours under his hand, as if delivered to him at Paris by the King's order, so that when the pursuer came to be included in the Marquis of Montrose's capitulation, General Monck and Colonel Cobbet were very close and severe upon him, but he producing Middleton's receipt, and standing to it with a firm countenance and exact answers, he was included in the capitulation, and thus the Honours were also secured till the King's restoration in the year 1660. At which time the Countess of Marschall writes to the King to know his pleasure about the Honours, and had a very kind return of thanks for her good service, with orders to deliver the Honours to the Earl Marschall, Lord Privy Seal, but also gave the pursuer the patent of Knight Marschall, with are honourable fee, and both in that patent and in the pursuer's parent, as Earl of Kintore, his foresaid service and preservation of the Honours is very honourably narrated, and the Lord Lyon was appointed to give the pursuer Crown, Sceptre and Sword, as additions to his coat of arms. Notwithstanding whereof, the said Sir George Ogilvy, not content with the acknowledgements he might pretend to for the small service he had done in the said matter, and which acknowledgement was also bestowed upon him, by his being made a Knight Baronet, and receiving some other reward and marks of his royal favour, had yet the confidence to send up his son, now the said Sir William, to London about the same time, and arrogating to himself the sole preservation of the Honours, and making his address to his Majesty by the Lord Ogilvie, thereafter Earl of Airly, the Countess Marschall was necessitate to send to London a gentleman express, and also to give a true information of the whole matter to the Earl of Middleton for repressing Sir George his foresaid presumption and arrogance, which was accordingly done.

For the Earl of Middleton having represented the affair to the King, his Majesty refused to give any more ear to Sir George's false suggestions, which put an end to that attempt. If Sir George had kept himself within bounds, neither the Countess of Marschall, who had that concern for him as to recommend him to his Majesty's favour, nor any of the family of Marschall would have grudged him the just reward of his faithful and discreet service, but his arrogant impudence to have the whole care and good service of having preserved the Honours ascribed to himself, with some other practises used at home for that effect, and thereby designing to rob the Earls of Marschall and the pursuer of their true merit and belie his Majesty's Patent, was that which justly offended.

But though Sir George was put to silence, and did for many years thereafter content himself with the reward he had got without pretending any further, yet the said Sir William, his son, has of late had the confidence to cause print and publish a most foolish and reproachful pamphlet, thereby reflecting on the memory of the said Countess of Marschall. He also presumes openly to cast all the reproach and disgrace he can upon the pursuer, as if he had falsely ascribed to himself a concern and interest in preserving the said Honours and thereby surprised the King, and got from him places and patents which he had no pretence to.

For in his foresaid villainous pamphlet, page tenth and eleventh, he says that the old Countess Marschall wrote to the King that her son John Keith (now the pursuer) had preserved the Honours, though, he says, that the pursuer was then abroad, and knew nothing of the matter, and then adds that the King, knowing nothing of Sir George and his mother's service, in respect they did not timely apply, did, upon the said Countess's misrepresentation, create her son first Knight Marschall and then Earl of Kintore, and ordered him a pension, for his pretended preservation of the Honours. And then this pamphlet gives an account how the said Sir George practised the said minister, Mr James Grainger and got the Sceptre from him, and likewise surprised the Earl Marschall to give him a receipt of the whole Honours, as if these had been parts of his good services, whereas it's known, and can be made appear by write under the Mr Grainger's hand, that both these attempts were fraudulent and purposely designed to support these false pretentions which the father Sir George did long since so impudently set up.

And now the son doth no less insolently boast of, and this does most falsely and basely defame and reproach the pursuer, by offering to rob him of his just merits and honour, and likewise to belie his Majesty's patents in favour of the pursuer, and throw the blackest slander upon the pursuer's name, honour, and fame. All which being evidently made out by the said pamphlet, whereof a printed copy is herewith produced in the clerk's hands, it is clear that the foresaid Sir William is guilty airt and pairt of a most injurious defamation and atrocious slander, which he ought not only to be made to retract as a manifest villainy, but likewise he ought to be further punished in his person and goods, at the sight of the Lords of her Majesty's Privy Counsel, to the example and terror of others to commit the like in time coming. As also the foresaid ignominious pamphlet ought to be burnt by the hand of the hangman, and all other reparation made to the said pursuer of his honour and good name, that can be proper against such an injurious and reproachful undertaking.

And about the charge given to the said defender to have compered before the Lords of Privy Counsel, at a certain day bygone, to have answered to the points of the foresaid complaints, and to have heard and seen such order and course taken thereabout as the Lords of Privy Counsel should have thought fit under the pain of rebellion, and putting of them to the horn, with certification, as in the said principal libel and executions thereof at more length is contained. Which libel being upon the day and date of these presents, called in presence of the said Lords of Privy Counsel. And the said pursuer compearing personally at the bar with Sir James Stewart, her Majesty's Advocate, Sir David Dalrymple and Mr William Carmichael, her Majesty's Solicitor, Mr Robert Forbes. Mr William Black, and Mr Patrick Leith, his advocates. And the said Sir William Ogilvy, defender, being oft times called, and not compearing personally, but by Sir David Thoires, Sir David Cunninghame, Mr Francis Grant, and Mr Mungo Carnegie, his advocates, who produced two testificats, one of them under the hands of Mr Alexander Thomson, Doctor of Medicine at Montrose, wherein he declares on soul and conscience, that the defender, Sir William Ogilvy is under such a weakness arid indisposition of body, that he cannot travel to Edinburgh without manifest danger of his life. And the other under the hands of the minister and the elder of the Parish of Kinneff, wherein they also declare that he has been valetudinary for these several years bygone, and particularly since Martinmass last, to the best of their knowledge and skill, and that he is so weak, that he cannot travel to Edinburgh without manifest hazard of his life. Both dated at Barrass the twenty-sixth of June, seventeen hundred and two years.

And the pursuer, to verify and instruct his libel, produced a patent of honour under his Majesty's great seal, creating him Knight Marschall of the kingdom of Scotland, for the causes within and therein specified, dated at the Court of Whitehall, the second day of January sixteen hundred and sixty-six years. As also produced a pamphlet, entitled 'Ane true Accompt of the Preservation of the Regalia of Scotland, viz. the Croun, Sceptre, and Sword, from falling into the hands of the English Usurpers, by Sir George Ogilvy of Barras, Knight and Baronet'.

As also a receipt granted by Mr James Grainger, minister at Kinneff, to the Countess Marschall, bearing him to have in his custody the Honours of the kingdom, viz. the Crown, Sceptre, and Sword, and where the same were absconded that the said Countess might have access thereto. Dated the thirty-first day of March sixteen hundred and fifty-two years. And likewise produced a Declaration under the said Mr James Grainger's hand, about the way and manner of preserving of the Honours by the Countess Marschall, dated the nineteenth day of October, sixteen hundred and sixty years, with a missive letter from the said minister to the said Countess Marschall, dated the twelfth of November, sixteen hundred and sixty; with another letter from the Earl of Middleton to the said Countess Marschall, dated the fifteenth of November sixteen hundred and sixty, with two letters from his Majesty King Charles the Second to the said Countess Marschall, the one whereof, dated the fourth of January sixteen hundred and fifty-five, and the other the fourth of September sixteen hundred and sixty. And the libel, testificats produced for the defender, patent of honour, pamphlet, receipt and instructions above mentioned, being fully read in presence of his Grace, Her Majesty's High Commissioner, and the Lords of her Majesty's Privy Counsel, and they having duly considered the same, His Grace Her Majesty's High Commissioner, and the Lords of Her Majesty's Privy Counsel, ordain the said pamphlet as injurious, ignominious and villainous, defaming the said Earl of Kintore, pursuer, to be burnt by the hands of the common hangman of the burgh of Edinburgh, at the Crosse of the said burgh upon Friday next, being the tenth instant, betwixt the hours of eleven and twelve in the forenoon. And ordains the Magistrates of Edinburgh to see the same effectual and put to due execution upon the said day, as they will be answerable. And, in respect of the certificates produced, continue the process against the defender as to the personal conclusion against him and the other points contained in the libel until the sixteenth of July instant.

22 – ACT IN FAVOUR OF THE EARL OF KINTORE, FOR A DILIGENCE TO CITE WITNESSES.

Edinburgh, 23 July 1702.

About the Petition given in and presented to the Lords of his Majesty's Privy Council by John Earl of Kintore, Showing: That where the petitioner having raised a complaint against Barrass, elder and younger, for printing, publishing, and dispersing a most defamatory pamphlet, and the same being called, there is a testificate produced for old Barrass of his inability to travel, and the young man denied the libel.

When this complaint was raised, the Earl of Kintore did not so much as think that a thing so palpable would have been denied and at first had no design of citing any witnesses. And these few that were cited at random, whereof only three have compered, and a second diligence granted against the other two, so that is most necessary that the petitioner be allowed a new diligence for citing of some more witnesses who may clearly prove the matter of fact contained in the libel.

And seeing the committee have not yet met, and none of the witnesses have yet deponed, and that the granting of their diligence will nowise protract but further the process, and bring it to a conclusion, and therefore craving to the effect after mentioned as the said petition bears, the Lords of his Majesty's Privy Counsel having considered this petition given in to them by John Earl of Kintore, they hereby grant and allow to the said petitioner, a diligence for citing of witnesses to compear before their Lordships, and depone in the within process, and the Council assigns the twenty eight day of July instant for that effect.

23 – DECREE: THE EARL OF KINTORE AGAINST OGILVY OF BARRASS.

About the libel or letters of complaint raised and pursued before the Lords of her Majesty's Privy Council, at the instance of John Earl of Kintore, Knight Marschall of her Majesty's ancient kingdom of Scotland, with concourse of Sir James Stewart, her Majesty's advocate for her Highness's interest in the matter under written. Making mention, that where every man's honour ought to be dear to him as his life, and that any injury by way of defamation in point of truth and honour, and tending to rob any person thereof, specially where his truth and honour is concerned in the most delicate and tender matters, is a most atrocious injury, not only most sensible to the persons injured, but aiming to expose him in the view and construction of all men, and therefore by the law of this and all other well-governed realms, most severely punishable.

Nevertheless, it is of verity, that Sir William Ogilvy of Barrass, and David Ogilvy, his son, are guilty of the foresaid crime of defamation, and that in the most injurious and insolent manner, in so far as Sir George Ogilvie, father to the said Sir William, having been bred and brought up from a very low and obscure beginning by the deceast Earl Marschall and his family and having, about sixteen hundred and fifty one, been made lieutenant of the garrison of Dunnottar by the said Earl, the keeper of the said castle. By this means, the Honours of the said kingdom, viz. the Crown, Sceptre, and Sword, which, by King Charles the Second, when at that time being in England, were committed to the said Earl, to be secured in the said Castle of Dunnottar, fell to be in some manner under the charge of the said Sir George, according to the trust the Earl had reposed in him.

But the Earl having lodged the Honours in a secret place of the castle, and thereafter coming unluckily to be surprised, with several other noblemen, at Elliot, and with them made prisoner and carried to London, he was necessitated to send his private order, with the keys of that secret place where the Honours were, which he always kept about him, to the Countess of Marschall, his mother, praying her to take care of the Honours, it being no more in his power to look after them. Whereupon, she entrusted them to the care and keeping of the said Sir George as lieutenant of the place as said is who, though he received the said trust, proved very unlucky in it, if the said Earl of Kintore, pursuer, then Mr John Keith, had not, (albeit very young), by a happy foresight, prevented the great hazard, in as much as when the Committee of Estates had, about that time, ordered the Lord Balcarras to receive the Honours out of the castle of Dunnottar, and the said Sir George was very much afraid to deny the Committee's order. Yet the said pursuer, apprehending the danger, refused to give them out to the said Earl of Balcarras, which did very visibly in the event prevent their falling into the hand of the English, when within a little thereafter the English became masters of all Scotland.

The Honours having thus escaped this hazard, were still kept in the castle, but the English marching northward toward Dunnottar, the foresaid Countess ordered the Honours to be conveyed privately out of the way, which was done a few days thereafter, by the very faithful assistance of one Mr James Grainger, minister at Kinneff, who, by his wife and his maid, caused bring the Honours in a bundle of flax to his own house, and then lodged them in the kirk, with a very exact caution, and gave the Countess of Marschall a receipt bearing particularly the place of the kirk where they were hid, and which indeed was the security of the Honours, through the good conduct of the Countess and the good service of the said minister and his wife, during the whole time of the English usurpation.

For the English thereafter having besieged Dunnottar, it was surrendered by Sir George, the lieutenant, upon a very mean capitulation, and the lieutenant was thereby bound to deliver the Honours, or give a rational account of them, whereupon, when Sir George and his wife were required, they asserted that the Honours were carried abroad by the pursuer and delivered to the King at Paris, which was indeed the contrivance that the pursuer had then advised, and the principal cause of his going abroad; but Sir George not having, at that time, got the Earl's declaration from Paris, he and his wife were kept prisoners until the Earl wrote home from Paris, owning that he had the Honours and delivered them as said is, which proved the means of the said Sir George's liberation.

But the Earl having this far concerned himself for the preservation of the Honours, he was constrained to remain abroad for fear of the English, until the Earl of Middleton came over to Scotland, and then the pursuer accompanied him in that expedition, in which he met with several hardships, being at first taken by the English, and then constrained to join with General Middleton and the rest, in the hills until they were all defeated, at which time the pursuer foreseeing his danger, fell upon a happy contrivance, both for the security of his own person and likewise, the safety of the honours. For General Middleton being to leave Scotland, the pursuer took a receipt of the Honours under his hand, as delivered to him at Paris by the King's order, so that when the pursuer came to be included in the Marquis of Montrose's capitulation, General Monck and Colonel Cobbet were very close and severe upon him. But he producing Middleton's receipt, and standing to it with a firm countenance and exact answers, he was included in the capitulation, and thus the Honours were also secured, until the King's restoration, in the year sixteen hundred and sixty, at which time, the Countess of Marschall writes to the King to know his pleasure about the Honours, and had a very kind return of thanks for her good service, with orders to deliver the Honours to the Earls Marschall.

And the King being informed of what had passed, as is above narrated, he not only made the Earl of Marschall Lord Privy Seal, but also gave to the pursuer the patent of Knight Marschall, with an honourable fee. And both in that patent, and in the pursuers patent as Earl of Kintore, his foresaid service and preservation of the Honours is very honourably narrated, and the Lord Lyon was appointed to give the pursuer the Crown, Sceptre, and Sword, as an addition to his coat of arms. Notwithstanding whereof, the foresaid Sir George Ogilvie, not content with the acknowledgement that he might pretend to for the small service he had done in the said matter, and which acknowledgement was also bestowed upon him by his being made a Knight Baronet, and receiving some other rewards and remarks of his royal favour, had yet the confidence to send up his son, now the said Sir William Ogilvy, to London, about the same time, and arrogating to himself the sole preservation of the Honours, and making his address to his Majesty by the Lord Ogilvy, thereafter Earl of Airly, the Countess Marschall was necessitated to send to London a gentleman express, and also to give a true information of the whole matter to the Earl of Middleton, for repressing Sir George his foresaid presumption and arrogance, which was accordingly done. For the Earl of Middleton having represented the affair to the King, his Majesty refused to give any more ear to Sir George's false suggestions, which put an end to that attempt.

If Sir George had kept himself within bounds, neither the Countess Marschall, who had that concern for him as to recommend him to his Majesty's favour, nor any of the family of Marschall, would have grudged him the just reward of his faithful and discreet service, but his arrogant impudence to have the whole care and good service of having preserved the Honours ascribed to himself, with some other practices used at home for that effect, and thereby designing to rob the Earls of Marschall and the pursuer of their true merit, and belie his Majesty's patent, was that which justly offended.

But though Sir George was put to silence and did for many years thereafter content himself with the reward he had got without pretending any further, yet the said Sir William, his son, and David Ogilvy, his grandchild, have of late had the confidence to cause print and publish a most foolish and reproachful pamphlet, whereby reflecting on the memory of the said Countess of Marschall. They also presume openly to cast all the reproach and disgrace they can upon the pursuer, as if he had falsely ascribed to himself a concern and interest in preserving the said Honours, and thereby surprised the King, and got from him places and patents which he had no pretence to.

For in their foresaid villainous pamphlet, page tenth and eleventh, they say that the old Countess wrote to the King, that her son, John Keith (now the pursuer), had preserved the Honours, though they say that the pursuer was then abroad, and knew nothing of the matter; and then add, that the King, knowing nothing of Sir George and his wife's service, in respect they did not timely apply, did, upon the said Countess's misrepresentation, create her son first Knight Marschall and then Earl of Kintore, and ordered him a pension for his pretended preservation of the Honours. And then this pamphlet gives an account, how the said Sir George practised the said minister, Mr James Grainger, and got the Sceptre from him and, likewise, surprised the Earl Marschall to give him a receipt of the whole Honours, as if these had been parts of his good services.

Whereas it is known, and can be made appear by write, under Mr James Grainger's hand, that both these attempts were fraudulent, and purposely designed to prevent [sic] these false pretentions, which the father, Sir George, did so impudently set up, and now the son and grandchild do no less insolently boast of.

And this does most falsely and basely reproach and defame the pursuer, by offering to rob him of his just merit and honour; and likewise to belie his Majesty's patents in favour of the pursuer, and through the blackest slander upon the pursuers name, honour and fame. All which being evidently made out by the said pamphlet, whereof a printed copy is herewith produced in the Clerk's hands, it is clear that the foresaid Sir William and David Ogilvies are guilty airt and pairt of the most injurious defamation and atrocious slander, which they ought not only to be made to retract as a manifest villainy but, likewise, they ought to be further punished in their persons and goods at the sight of the Lords of Privy Council, to the example and terror of others to commit the like in time coming; as also the foresaid ignominious pamphlet ought to be burnt by the hand of the hangman, and all other reparation made to the said pursuer of his honour, fame and good name, that can be proper against such an injurious and reproachful undertaking.

And about the charge given to the whole forenamed defenders to have compered personally at a certain day bygone, before the said Lords of Privy Council, to have answered to the points of the foresaid complaint, and to have heard and seen such order and course taken thereabout as the said Lords should have thought fit, under the pain of rebellion, and putting of them to the horn, with certification, as is in the said principle libel and executions thereof at more length is contained; which libel being upon the twenty-first of July called in presence of the said Lords of her Majesty's Privy Council, and the said Earl of Kintore, pursuer, compearing personally with Sir James Stewart, her Majesty's advocate, Sir David Dalrymple, Mr William Carmichael, Mr Robert Forbes, Mr William Black, and Mr Patrick Leith, advocates, his prosecutors.

And the said David Ogilvy, one of the defenders, compearing also personally at the bar with Sir David Thoirs, Sir David Cunningham, and Mr Francis Grant, advocates, his prosecutors, who at the bar, declared and owned the pamphlet within libelled on to be injurious, ignominious, and villainous, defaming the said Earl of Kintore; and that this defender at the bar would disown the same, and that he had no concern therein: And the said David Ogilvy, as said is, being present at the bar, and he being enquired at if he owned and adhered to what his said advocates had declared, he answered that he did adhere to what his said prosecutors had said in his name, who also produced a certificate and declaration upon soul and conscience, subscribed by Mr Alexander Thomson, Doctor of Medicine, wherein he declares that the other defender, Sir William Ogilvy, is not able to travel to Edinburgh without endangering his life, in respect of his indisposition and weakness of body.

And the said libel being read, and both parties prosecutors fully heard at the bar, the said Lords have admitted, and hereby admit the same to probation; and the witnesses cited being called, compered at the bar as marked in the roll did make faith, the Council nominates and appoints the Earls of Marr, Levan, and Hyndford, Viscount of Tarbat, and Lord Forbes, and Lord Provost of Edinburgh, to be a committee to examine the witnesses, and recommends to the said committee to meet tomorrow at ten in the forenoon, and declares any two of them a quorum, and reserves all objections against the said witnesses to be discussed before the said committee, and grants letters of second diligence against the witnesses cited and not compering as they are marked in the roll, and assigns the ... day of ... next to come for that effect.

And the witnesses having compered, deponed in manner mentioned in their oaths and depositions. And the said Lords of Privy Council having this day advised the process at the instance of the said John Earl of Kintore against the said Sir William Ogilvy of Barrass, and David Ogilvy, younger thereof, his son; and the said Lords having heard and considered the depositions of the witnesses adduced in the said matter, read in their presence, and having also considered the said libel and whole steps of the process, and the information for both parties in the said process being fully read, and the said Lords finds the said libel sufficiently proven against the said David Ogilvy, one of the defenders;

And the said Lords have fined and amerciated, and hereby fines and amerciates, the said David Ogilvie, younger of Barrass, one of the defenders, in the source of twelve hundred pounds Scots; and have decerned and ordained, and hereby decerns and ordains, the said David Ogilvy, defender, to make payment of the said source of twelve hundred pounds money foresaid to the said John Earl of Kintore, pursuer for the expenses and damages he has sustained, and ordains the said David Ogilvy, defender, to be committed prisoner to the Edinburgh tollbooth, therein to remain, ay and while the said defender makes payment of the said sum to the said pursuer, as said is, or give sufficient security to the said John Earl of Kintore for the same, and further to remain therein during the Council's pleasure; and the said Lords give orders and warrant to macer of Privy Council, or messengers at arms, and ordains and requires all Sheriffs of shires and their deputies, and other magistrates and ministers of the law to search for, take, and apprehend and commit to prison, the person of the said David Ogilvie, younger of Barrass, prisoner to any tollbooth within the kingdom, therein to remain, ay and while he makes payment, or give security and satisfaction as above, and during the Committee's farther pleasure thereabout; and ordains letters of horning on fifteen days, and others needful, to be directed hereon in form as appropriate.

24 – OGILVY'S ANSWERS TO THE PROCESS.

An Account of the Process raised before the Privy Council of Scotland, anno 1702, by John Earl of Kintore against Sir William Ogilvy of Barrass and his eldest Son, the present Sir David Ogilvy. And to put the same in a true and genuine light, I do fairly and candidly oppose Kintore's allegations first in his libel and secondly in his scurrilous paper called Ane Information. This I presume will fully satisfy and disabuse all the unbiased and unprejudiced and put a curb upon the foul mouthed, and will let the world know how and by whom the Regalia of Scotland were kept and preserved from falling into the hands of Oliver Cromwell the usurper.

Contraria juxta se posita magis elucescunt.

1) Whereas the Earl of Kintore says that every man's honour ought to be dear to him as his life, and an injury by way of defamation in point of truth and honour as concerned in the most delicate and tender matters is a most atrocious injury &c and alleges that the said Sir William Ogilvy is guilty of the foresaid crime of defamation and also says that his father Sir

George was bred and brought up from a low and obscure beginning by the deceast Earl Marschall and in his family.

To all which 'tis answered that the said Sir William Ogilvy his causing publish to the world a true account of the preservation of the Regalia of Scotland, viz. Crown Sword and Sceptre by his father Sir George Ogilvy and Dame Elizabeth Douglas his mother, and by asserting and vindicating their loyalty and sufferings by clear process and authentic documents which undeniably prove the truth of what is asserted, how and by whom the matter was contrived and acted.

I say for the said Sir William his causing publish a true account of the preservation of the Regalia, ut supra, cannot be reckoned defamation or any injury against the Earl of Kintore since 'tis plain that any relation given resolves into a proper self defence of Sir George and his lady's memory and of the only reward that was left their family, namely, the honour thereof, and that by no more than telling the truth of a history in so far as it did appear by adminicles in write which takes off all animus injuriandi and purges the presumption of offending.

And as to what is alleged anent Sir George his being bred and brought up in the Earl Marschall's family. 'Tis answered that the said Sir George Ogilvy was brought up and educated as a gentleman by his own parents and in their family and, for instance, that Sir George, his father, had then a competency to live creditably as a gentleman and did educate his only son and child accordingly he having the wodsett of Lumghair being than 9 chalders of victual from the said Earl of Kintore's father and as much money upon bank as he had upon that wodsett, and that Sir George had a fortune of his own is evident by his having a post in the military as Cornet of Horse designing him of Pitdowie (which was a piece of heritage he had then in the shire of Angus). The commission is dated at Aberdeen, 22nd July 1640, and is yet extant, and the Earl Marschall's second Commission to the said Sir George designs him of Barrass and lieutenant governor of Dunnottar Castle.

And the Earl Marschall never used the said Sir George but as a gentleman which truly he was, and the said Sir George was on all occasions, during the whole series of his life, most ready to serve the Earl

Marschall and was always esteemed by him as one of his special friends and trustees. And for his prudence fidelity and integrity the said Earl was pleased to make use of his advice and assistance in the management of his affairs and concerns of the greatest moment, as is evident by many missive letters yet extant from the said Earl which do him the honour to bear several expressions of great intimacy and respect. For instance, I shall insert the purport of some of them particularly one from Kendal in England, dated the 4th August 1648 wherein his Lordship writes to Sir George 'According to my promise I will write to you with every occasion. I came yesternight to the army, the 3 instant, where I found them at Kendall. The morrow or next day we are to march to Lancashire. Our army are all in good health and heartily received by the country. Lambert is lying 26 miles below us at Barnie Castle in Yorkshire also Sir Marmaduke Langdale is marched for joining with our friends there. If once your harvest were done I hope you will be as good as your word and come and see us, when I promise you an excellent tower and merry days by the grace of God. Remember me to all friends and to your wife father and mother.' And so his Lordship concludes 'Directed for his loving friend George Ogilvy of Barrass.' In another letter when my Lord Marschall was prisoner at London, dated the 26 November 1656, his Lordship was pleased to express himself to the said Sir George. 'In the first place you might give me leave to wish you joy in your new wife and I pray God bless you both and grant she fill the room of the other which I hope she will do for I hear she is a good woman.' And his Lordship after the imparting of some business adds 'I hope to be thankful to all I have found kind to me and particularly to yourself and I trust in God to be merry at your fireside, till then and still, I am Your most affectionate and Directed, ut supra. Assured friend, – Sic subscribitur, Marschall'

There's another letter which does farther evidence my Lord Marschall's respect to Sir George dated 23 December 1657 wherein his Lordship is pleased to thank Sir George for his advice in some affair and concludes, 'I will expect you here at Inverugie, till then and ever I will be Your loving friend to his uttermost, – Sic subscribitur, Marschall'

'My wife and I are your and your wife's servants and we will drink your grandchild's health the morrow.' Directed for my worthy friend George Ogilvy of Barrass.

There's another letter from the Earl Marschall to Sir George, dated at Newcastle 25 May, 1657, wherein his Lordship says in the last paragraph and close of his letter 'You have already given such proofs of your respect and kindness to me as I shall not doubt but now in this nick of time when my all lies at the stake you will continue your wonted favours to me so be assured whatever shall be my condition I shall ever acknowledge myself to be – Yours &c.'

There are other two letters from the Earl Marschall to Sir George, dated after King Charles II's restoration and after that the said John Earl of Kintore had set up his pretensions as the preserver of the Honours of Scotland. The first letter is dated at Whitehall 8 January, 1663, as follows:

'I received yours and am vexed that any having although relation or kindness to me should scruple at your offering your endeavour for my good. I am, believe me, sorry they are so biased and be you assured I respect your kindness and do desire you will continue to be so still I am, – Yours &c. Directed for my worthy friend Sir George Ogilvy of Barrass.'

The other letter is dated Whitehall, 10 February 1663 as follows:

'I have sent home my servant Ramsey to show my friends our resolution of coming to Scotland in the end of May or beginning of June and shall not doubt of your concurring with my friends for so good an end.'

Now to return to the allegations;

2) 'Tis alleged in the Earl of Kintore's libel that when the Honours were committed to the said Earl Marschall to be secured and kept in the Castle of Dunnottar that they (the honours) fell to be in some manner under the charge of the said Sir George according to the trust the Earl Marschall had reposed in him, and that the Earl Marschall having lodged the honours in a secret place of the castle and he being thereafter

unluckily made prisoner and carried to London he was necessitated to send private orders with the keys of the place where the Honours lay (which he always kept about him) to his mother the Countess Marschall praying her to take care of the Honours, it being no more in his power to look after them, and that she did then entrust them to the care and keeping of the said Sir George; and that he had proved very unlucky in it, if that the now Earl of Kintore had not prevented the hazard by his foresight, in as much as, when the Committee of Estates had ordered the Lord Balcarras to receive the honours out of the said Castle, and that the said Sir George was afraid to deny the Committee's order, yet the now Earl of Kintore, though then very young, did refuse to give them out of the castle and that his doing of this did prevent their falling in the enemy's hands when within a little while they, the English, became masters of all Scotland except the said castle wherein the Honours were kept; and that when they were marching northward towards Dunnottar the foresaid Countess ordered the Honours to be conveyed privately out of the way which was done within a few days by the assistance of Mr Grainger, his wife and maid, and were carried in a bundle of flax to the Kirk of Kinneff and hidden therein; and that the minister gave the said Countess a receipt bearing the place of the Kirk where they were hidden whereby the Honours were secured through the good conduct of the Countess and by the assistance of the said minister, his wife and maid during the whole time of Cromwell's usurpation.

To all which it is answered that 'tis neither probable nor feasible that the said Earl Marschall did keep or withhold from the said Sir George (then governor of the said castle) the key of that secret place where the Honours were than kept and secured, in regard the said Earl's commission to Sir George as his lieutenant gives unto him the sole power and command of the house and castle of Dunnottar under his Lordship whereby it doth justly and reasonably appear that since the said Sir George had the keeping and sole power of the said castle he had also absolute and full power of the Honours.

For the Earl Marschall having reposed such entire confidence in Sir George (beyond all his Lordships friends at that juncture and nick of time) 'tis not to be doubted but the Honours were primarily and particularly entrusted to him at the receiving of his commission. And it doth farther appear by the Earl of Loudoun, then Chancellor of Scotland, his missive letter to which I refer, that the said Sir George had the immediate and particular trust of the said Honours from the Earl Marschall and none other, and his Lordship being then prisoner at London the said Sir George had the sole care and disposal of the Honours and was accountable for them, and it's hereby evident that the said Earl of Kintore had no trust, care of, or concern with the said castle or the Honours.

That the Committee of Estates ordered Sir George Ogilvy (then governor of the said castle) to deliver up the honours to Balcarras is evident by his Lordships missive letter to which I refer, but that the late John, Earl of Kintore gave advice about the securing of them or dissuaded Sir George the then governor, from giving out the Honours to Balcarras is no better than a jest both upon the account of the Earl of Kintore's being then very young (as he himself acknowledges) and therefore very unfit to give counsel in a matter of so great importance at such a critical juncture, and moreover, 'twas notourly known that the said Sir George was one of the most prudent and foreseeing men of that age and his conduct did bespeak him such for if he had obeyed the order of the then Committee of Estates seconded by verbal and literal solicitation from the Lord Balcarras then the honours had inevitably fallen in the hands of Oliver Cromwell, and that the said Earl of Kintore gave advice thereabout far less refused to give the Honours out of the castle does not at all appear nor can be proven any other way than by a bare assertion and licet omnibus allegare, but that the Honours were not delivered to Balcarras is most certain as the event hath proven for exitus acta probat.

The said Sir George having the weighty charge of the government of the said castle and the preservation of the Honours, did communicate his anxiety to his lady and upon a serious consultation between them it was concluded she should convey the honours out of the said castle and secure them without her husband's knowledge, which she bravely undertook and did wisely and happily effect and stood the shock of all the menaces and maltreatment of the enemy with such a firm and undaunted resolution and constancy as is rarely to be paralleled in one of her sex. And the truth of this is evident by Major Deane's warrant for her and her said husband's release upon bail, as above narrated. And he is so far from being satisfied or soothed up by the evasion she made that he touches it only in general terms superficially and without much regard, the words being these: 'And lastly said his wife had conveyed them (meaning the Honours) to a gentleman who carried them to foreign parts. I am willing in case he shall procure good security of 2000 or 1500 lib. ster. that he shall render himself a true prisoner to you upon demand as also that his wife shall do the likes &c.'

Now what would have made Maj. Gen. Deane express himself so if Sir George his lady had not bold owned and maintained that she had conveyed out and secured the honours as aforesaid? And if she had not been the main actrix in contriving the manner of transporting and securing the honours and the only person who entrusted them to the said ministers wife what motive could have induced her to have undergone a long and strait imprisonment jointly with her husband and to have suffered so much both in her person and estate. Sure, not to procure wealth and honour to the then Mr John Keith late Earl of Kintore (too great a compliment to bestow) but out of an innate principle, like the brave old Earls of Douglas her predecessors, of loyalty and fidelity to her prince and out of a just regard to the honour of that kingdom which then lay at stake, and in hopes that her family and posterity should have reaped and enjoyed a reward suitable to such an honourable merit.

And at the time that Sir George's lady sent for Mr Grainger's wife and entrusted the hiding and securing of the honours to her as aforesaid it is not probable that the then Countess of Marschall had then any acquaintance of the said minister or his wife, though it's incontrovertibly true that Sir George Ogilvy had been and his grandson Sir David Ogilvy is yet in possession of the lands of Barrass lying in the parish of Kinneff where Mr Grainger was minister, and consequently Sir George's lady could not but know the minister's wife and having experienced her fidelity and honesty in other things did the more freely adventure to entrust her with matters of so great importance, but that the Countess of Marschall did entrust the hiding and securing of the honours to the said Minister and his wife doth not appear to any rational unbiased unprejudiced person. Her ladyship having no concern in that parish it can't be supposed that she could then be intimate with nor repose such confidence in the said minister and his wife especially she (the Countess) having churches much nearer to the place, I mean Dunnottar Castle, of which the Earl Marschall is patron, and therefore 'tis to be thought that the Countess would have committed the Honours rather to the care and custody of some of the ministers of these churches, if to any at all, where she had interest.

3). 'Tis alleged in the Earl of Kintore's libel that the said Sir George made an ill defence of and surrendered the said Castle upon a very mean capitulation. To which it is answered that it's well known to all that 'twas the last castle held out that time and that against such a prevailing army that if Sir George had not been a man of extraordinary conduct and courage he could not have stood out so long as he did, which is evident by the missive letters from some of the commanders in chief of the enemy. as follows:

[introduced previously]
8 November 1651, General Overton, for the Honourable Governor of Dunnottar Castle.
22 November 1651, Colonel Dutton, for the Commander in Chief of Dunnottar Castle.

Sir George's return seems to answer both though 'tis directed to Dutton. And for the then Earl Marschall's personal safety, he being in the enemy's hands, as well as for the preservation of his houses and lands from damage makes these officers believe he had his commission absolutely from the King, and to speak freely though Sir George had his commission at first from and under the then Earl Marschall (whose merit was very great) yet as appears by the then Chancellor and the then Lord Balcarras letters, if the Regalia or honours had fallen in the hands of the enemy Sir George and he only would have been accountable for them (after his disobeying the order of the Committee of Estates) both to King and Kingdom.

The Copy of Sir George's answer to these letters is as follows (though directed to Dutton):

22 November 1651, George Ogilvy to Colonel Dutton [ibid.]

There's another letter as follows:

3 January 1652, Dundee, – G. Lambert for The Governor of Dunnottar Castle.

'Sir, – being desirous to avoid the effusion of blood and the destroying of the Country I have thought fit to send you this summons to surrender up the Castle of Dunnottar, with the provisions of war thereto belonging, into my hands for the use of the Parliament of the Commonwealth of England. If you shall hearken hereto with speed you shall have conditions for your self and the soldiers under your command as may befit a man of honour and one in your condition. I expect your speedy answer and am, Sir, Your servant, – sic subscribitur, G. Lambert.'

I shall add two letters more from Walley one of the enemy's commanders anent the exchange of prisoners.

10 & 15 February 1652, Aberdeen – General Walley to the Governor of the Castle of Dunnottar. [ibid.]

By all which it's evident that Sir George Ogilvy when governor of Dunnottar Castle could not have behaved himself better, and 'tis acknowledged by the said Earl of Kintore, in the reflective account he gave to Mr Alexander Nisbet to be printed in his book of heraldry, that there was then no hopes of succour nor the castle able to hold out long if once attacked.

And truly it's a wonder that it held out so long even until the 26 of May 1652 for there being no relief given and all hopes thereof then cut off and but thirty five men in the garrison, a mere handful in comparison of the number then requisite to defend the place, and all of them day and night upon duty were extremely fatigued and over-waked, yet they maintained their respective posts valorously for the space of ten days when closely besieged and from the enemy's leaguer [camp] at the Black Hill of Dunnottar were exposed to the havoc of bombs and the shocks of thundering cannon; and when the governor found that the garrison was not able to hold out longer and all forts within the kingdom being then reduced under command of the enemy, Sir George, the governor, judged it better to make a honourable capitulation then to have permitted the castle to have been stormed and when the garrison marched out with drums beating and colours flying and kindled matches for the space of a mile, the besiegers were astonished to admiration to see such a small force make so long and vigorous resistance against such a prevailing army. And the besiegers expressly told that if the castle had not been that day surrendered they were resolved to have stormed it the very next day following which easily they might have done considering the bad posture the garrison was in as aforesaid.

And that which some time before did mightily incommode Sir George, the governor, was a mutiny raised and fomented by one David Lighton who had been a colonel abroad yet by the said governor's diligence and conduct the mutiny was suppressed and crushed in the bud by causing train-out Colonel Lighton and never allowed him to re-enter the said castle whereby the soldiers were quashed and composed and the direful effects of that mutiny prevented which was to have sacrificed the governor and all under his charge to the merciless cruelty of the enemy. And 'twas a signal act of Providence that the design was discovered for there being several veteran soldiers in the garrison who had served in France and other places, most of them strangers to the governor and getting no pay from the public, made his post very uneasy and brought him to a deal of charges he being necessitated to give pay to the said Colonel Lighton, and to the surgeon, engineer and cannoneer, all out of his own estate, he having got no pay either for himself or them from the public.

4) 'Tis alleged in the said Earl of Kintore's libel that when Sir George and his lady were required by the English after the surrender of the Castle to deliver up the honours or give a rational account of them they asserted

that the honours were carried abroad by Mr John Keith, the said Earl of Kintore, and delivered by him to the King at Paris, and the Earl alleges that this was the contrivance he had devised and the principal cause of his going abroad.

To which 'tis answered that the said Earl of Kintore, at and before the time of conveying the honours out of the said castle knew nothing then how and by whom they were conveyed out and secured is doubly evident, first, by his account of that matter to Mr Nisbet to be insert in his book of heraldry, at Edinburgh, wherein the said Earl affirms that his mother the Countess of Marschall contrived the manner of securing of the honours and that she communicate the same to such a number of trusty persons as were requisite to make the design effectual among whom was George Ogilvy, a servant of the family, (who had been entrusted with the government of the castle), and that the design was the Honours should be conveyed out of the castle by sea and that accordingly they were carried to a church three miles distance.

By this it would also appear that the said Earl of Kintore had not got a right information (before or at the giving of this account to Mr Nisbet) how or after what manner the Honours were carried out of the said Castle. And the Earl further adds that his said mother ordered those she had entrusted with the carrying them off to give out and maintain (if the said castle should happen to be taken, on which was not much doubted) that her son John had carried them abroad and delivered them to the King then at Paris, and that she immediately wrote and acquainted her said son with the method she had taken, and desired he might own the same. This account to Mr Nisbet flatly contradicts the narrative of the said Earl's libel to the Privy-Council of Scotland and doth sufficiently prove that it was none of his contrivance, I mean the manner of preserving the said Honours and testimonium adversarii contra se est validissimum. Secondly, if the said Earl of Kintore had been then in Scotland, Sir George his lady could not have made use of his name by way of evasion for the enemy would have been soon undeceived.

5) It's alleged by the said Earl that by his firm countenance and exact answers when appearing before General Monk and Colonel Cobett, the

Honours were preserved till the King's restoration in the year 1660 at which time the Countess of Marschall writes to his Majesty to know his pleasure about the Honours, and that she had a very kind return of thanks with orders to deliver the honours to the Earl Marschall and that, the King being informed of what had passed as aforesaid, his Majesty gave the said Earl of Kintore (then Mr John Keith) the patent of Knight Marschall with a honourable fee.

To which it's answered that the said Sir George and his lady owned the having of the Honours, and his lady in particular constantly affirmed that she had sent them abroad as aforesaid to the King Charles the 2d, and so she and her husband stood in the gap and (next to the then Earl Marschall) suffered for all, and kept Mr Grainger the minister of Kinneff and his wife from being suspected, questioned, or known. And if the then Countess of Marschall got an order from the King to deliver the honours to the Earl Marschall why did she not deliver them accordingly? And moreover I must crave leave to say, with all due regard to her lady-ship's memory, that if my lady had entrusted the honours to Mr Grainger she would not have failed to have pursued him for delivering them to the said Sir George without her consent, and if her ladyship had given the trust of them at first to Sir George, and he meddling with the Honours to deliver them without her advice and concurrence, she would have pursued him for his intromission, but so it is she never intended any such action against any of them, since she could not prove that she had either entrusted the honours to Sir George or yet to Mr Grainger, which, if she could have done, there's no doubt she would have taken all redress law could have given her, for it's well known she was a very active and stirring lady.

6) The said Earl of Kintore alleges in his libel or Council letters that the said Sir George, not being content with the acknowledgements that he might pretend to for the small service he had done in the said mat-ter, had the confidence to send to London his son, Sir William Ogilvy, arrogating to himself the sole preservation of the honours, and making his address to his Majesty by the lord Ogilvy thereafter Earl of Airlie, the Countess of Marschall was necessitated to send to London a gentleman to

inform and desire the Earl of Middleton to repress Sir George's presumption and arrogance which was accordingly done and adds that the Earl of Middleton at the said Countess her solicitation did so represent the affair to the King Charles 2nd that his Majesty refused to give any more ear to Sir George's false suggestions which put an end to that attempt.

To which it's answered that the said Sir George was indeed frustrated of the just recompense and reward due to him and his lady by the opposition his son the late Sir William met with when at Court from those great minions to whom the matter was misrepresented, as aforesaid, both by the said Earl of Kintore his taking the start and by the endeavours used to prepossess both King and Court.

'Tis alleged in the Earl of Kintore's libel that, if the said Sir George had kept himself within bounds, neither the Countess nor any of the family of Marschall would have grudged him the just reward of his faithful service (this contradicts what the Earl of Kintore says as to the acknowledgements Sir George pretended for the small services he had done and is a convincing proof of Sir George his loyalty and fidelity) and then the said Earl goes on and says, 'but Sir George's arrogant impudence to have the whole care and good service of having preserved the honours ascribed to himself and thereby designed to rob the Earl Marschall and him of their true merit and also belie his Majesty's patents was that which justly offended, and that the said Sir George was put to silence and did for many years content himself with the reward he had got without pretending any further.'

To which it's answered that for the late Sir William Ogilvy of Barrass, his causing publish a true relation of the preserving and securing of the Regalia or Honours of Scotland, thereby to make known and perpetuate Sir George and his lady's good service and sufferings, and also to satisfy and disabuse this and neighbouring nations as to the manner how and the persons by whom that important matter was contrived carried on and happily effected, I say, cannot in law, equity and reason be constructed a design to rob the then Earl Marschall of his merit (whose loyalty and sufferings were such as no good man who loves his King and Country can question) for Sir George did rather add to and augment the

Earl Marschall's merit by discharging so handsomely and valiantly the trust the said Earl Marschall had honoured him with, which plainly and undeniably appears by a letter his Lordship sent Sir George from the Tower of London after the said castle was surrendered upon capitulation as aforesaid, in which letter, yet extant (as are all above mentioned), his Lordship expressly says these words, 'And though we have not obtained such as we could have wished yet, I must tell you that I will never be unmindful of your kindness expressed to me. Whenever it shall be in my power to let you know the same.'

This does further evidence that Sir George could not have done more at that time for the Earl Marschall's honour and interest than he did. But for my Lord Kintore to pretend that the Honours were preserved by him and his said mother only, to speak in his own words, was a plain robbing of the Earl Marschall of his merit and did prejudge the heir and representative of that family. And for the said Sir George or his son Sir William their using honest and lawful endeavours to obtain a reward and just recompense for the loyalty and sufferings of their family, as said is, and for Sir William Ogilvy his causing publish the same in defence of his family and posterity attacked, as aforesaid, by the said Earl of Kintore's unjust and reflective account of that matter to Mr Nisbet, professor of heraldry at Edinburgh, cannot be constructed a belying of his Majesty's patents or any just offence. And it's a rule both in law and nature that what truth the defender tells *ob propriam tutelam, id jure fecisse existimetur.*

And the doing of Sir George Ogilvy justice, as to his merit in preserving the Regalia, is so far from belying my Lord Kintore's patents that it is owned in King Charles II's patents of March 5 1661, whereby he creates George Ogilvy a Knight Baronet; its likewise owned in that prince's charter changing the ward holding of the lands of Barrass into that of blench, and it is again owned in the ratification of the same by Act of Parliament, so that his lordship, by denying Sir George's merit, contradicts them all three, which was certainly more criminal than what he unjustly charges upon Sir William and his son.

25 – ASSIGNATION OF A SEAT IN ARBROATH CHURCH TO CHRISTIAN GRANGER.

Assignation by Mr Patrick Strachan, Minister of Mains, and Lucras Granger, his spouse, to Christian Granger.

1710, July 25. Maines.- Be it known to all men be their presents, that whereas there being a seat in the church of Aberbrothick belonging to Mr John Granger, indweller there, and afterwards belonging to Mr Arthur Granger, minister of Panbryde, his eldest son, and now belonging to Lucras Grainger, eldest daughter to the said Mr Arthur Grainger, and spouse to Mr Patrick Strachan, minister at Maines, wherefore wit ye us, the said Maister Patrick Strachan and Lucras Grainger, his spouse, (having now undoubted right to that seat) for the love and favour we bear to Christian Grainger, lawful daughter to Mr John Grainger, minister at … , and grandchild to Mr James Grainger, minister at Kinneff, and for other onerous causes, good respects and considerations moving us, to have made, constitute and ordained, likeas we by these presents make, constitute and ordain the said Christian Grainger, her heirs and donators, our very lawful, undoubted, irrevocable sessioner and assignee in and to the foresaid seat in the Church of Aberbrothik, with full power to her and her foresaids to take possession thereof, and in case of opposition or any other taking violent possession, to pursue therefore as accords of the law, and generally to do every other thing we might have done ourselves before the granting hereof; turning and transferring the same and whole right thereof from us, our heirs, executors and all others our assignees, to and in favours of the said Christian Grainger and her foresaids, whom we, by their presents, surrogate and substitute in our full right, title, vice and place thereof for now and ever; obliging us, our heirs and executors to warrant their presents from our own proper fact and deed done or to be done in hurt and prejudice hereof solely; consenting to the registration hereof in the Books of Council and Session or of any other competent judicatory within the kingdom, and therein to remain for conservation, and, if need be, to receive execution as appropriate; and constitutes … our procurators, &c. In witness whereof (written be John Black, schoolmaster at Maines), we have subscribed these presents at Maines, the twenty fifth of July, one thousand seven hundred and ten, before these witnesses: John Scot, servitor to the said minister of Maines, Thomas Laurence, servitor to the Laird of Fentray, and John Black, writer hereof.

(Signed) Mr P. Strachane, Lucres Grainger, John Scot, witness, Thomas Laurance, witness, John Black, witness.

26 – SIR WALTER SCOTT'S LETTERS TO DR CROKER.

The bricked-up room that had held the Honours of Scotland since the Union of the Parliaments in 1707, was opened in 1818, due mainly to the efforts of Sir Walter Scott.

4 February 1818.

My dear Croker, – I have the pleasure to assure you the Regalia of Scotland were this day found in perfect preservation. The Sword of State and Sceptre showed marks of hard usage at some former period; but in all respects agree with the description in Thomson's work. I will send you a complete account of the opening tomorrow, as the official account will take some time to draw up. In the meantime, I hope you will remain as obstinate in your belief as St. Thomas, because then you will come down to satisfy yourself. I know nobody entitled to earlier information, save one, to whom you can perhaps find the means of communicating the result of our researches. The post is just going off. Ever yours truly, – Walter Scott

7 February 1818.

My dear Croker, – I promised I would add something to my report of yesterday, and yet I find I have but little to say. The extreme solemnity of opening sealed doors of oak and iron, and finally breaking open a chest which had been shut since 7th March 1707, about a hundred and eleven years, gave a sort of interest to our researches, which I can hardly express to you, and it would be very difficult to describe the intense eagerness with which we watched the rising of the lid of the chest, and the progress of the workmen in breaking it open, which was neither an easy nor a speedy task. It sounded very hollow when they worked on it with their tools, and I began to lean to your faction of the Little Faiths. However, I never could assign any probable or feasible reason for withdrawing these memorials of ancient independence; and my doubts rather arose from the conviction that many absurd things are done in public as well as in private life, merely out of a hasty impression of passion or resentment. For it was evident the removal of the Regalia might have greatly irritated people's minds here, and offered a fair pretext of breaking the Union, which for thirty years was the predominant wish of the Scottish nation.

The discovery of the Regalia has interested people's minds much more strongly than I expected, and is certainly calculated to make a pleasant and favourable impression upon them in respect to the kingly part of the constitution. It would be of the utmost consequence that they should be occasionally shown to them, under proper regulations, and for a small fee. The Sword of State is a most beautiful piece of workmanship, a present from Pope Julius II to James IV. The scabbard is richly decorated with filigree work of silver, double gilded, representing oak leaves and acorns, executed in a taste worthy that classical age in which the arts revived. A draughtsman has been employed to make sketches of these articles, in order to be laid before his Royal Highness.

The fate of these Regalia, which his Royal Highness's goodness has thus restored to light and honour, has on one or two occasions been singular enough. They were, in 1652, lodged in the Castle of Dunnottar, the seat of the Earl Marschall, by whom, according to his ancient privilege, they were kept. The castle was defended by George Ogilvie of Barrass, who, apprehensive of the progress which the English made in reducing the strong places in Scotland, became anxious for the safety of these valuable memorials. The ingenuity of his lady had them conveyed out of the castle in a bag on a woman's back, among some hards, as they are called, of lint. They were carried to the Kirk of Kinneff, and entrusted to the care of the clergyman named Grainger and his wife, and buried under the pulpit. The Castle of Dunnottar, though very strong and faithfully defended, was at length under necessity of surrendering, being the last strong place in Britain on which the royal flag floated in those calamitous times.

Ogilvie and his lady were threatened with the utmost extremities by the Republican General Morgan, unless they should produce the Regalia. The governor stuck to it that he knew nothing of them, as in fact they had been carried away without his knowledge. The lady maintained she had given them to John Keith, second son of the Earl Marschall, by whom, she said, they had been carried to France. They suffered a long imprisonment, and much ill usage.

On the Restoration, the old Countess Marschall, founding upon the story Mrs Ogilvie had told to screen her husband, obtained for her own son, John Keith, the Earldom of Kintore, and the post of Knight Marschall, with £400 a year, as if he had been in truth the preserver of the Regalia. It soon proved that this reward had been too hastily given, for Ogilvie of Barrass produced the Regalia, the honest clergyman refusing to deliver them to any one but those from whom he received them. Ogilvie was made a Knight Baronet, however, and got a new charter of the lands, acknowledging the good service. Thus it happened oddly enough, that Keith, who was abroad during the transaction, and had nothing to do with it, got the earldom, pension, &c., Ogilvie only inferior honours, and the poor clergyman nothing whatever, or, as we say, the hare's foot to lick.

As for Ogilvy's lady, she died before the Restoration, her health being ruined by the hardships she endured from the Cromwellian satellites. She was a Douglas, with all the high spirit of that proud family. On her deathbed, and not till then, she told her husband where the honours were concealed, charging him to suffer death rather than betray them. Popular tradition says, not very probably, that Grainger and his wife were booted (that is, tortured with the engine called the boots). I think that the Knight

Marschall's office rested in the Kintore family until 1715, when it was resumed on account of the bearded Earl's accession to the Insurrection of that year. He escaped well, for they might have taken his estate and his earldom. I must save post, however, and conclude abruptly. Yours ever, – Walter Scott

Index

If you are interested in purchasing other books published by Tempus,
or in case you have difficulty finding any Tempus books in your local bookshop,
you can also place orders directly through our website

www.tempus-publishing.com